Cndr Pettes

You, _____

can learn and teach valuable lessons from my

conversations with the "Dirty Dog."

Zig Ziglar

Eph 3 8-9

conversations
with my dog

zig ziglar

conversations
with my dog

BROADMAN
&HOLMAN
PUBLISHERS

Nashville, Tennessee

0-8054-3260-4

Published by Broadman & Holman Publishers,
Nashville, Tennessee

Dewey Decimal Classification: 248.84
Subject Headings: CHRISTIAN LIFE

Scripture quotations marked HCSB have been taken from the
Holman Christian Standard Bible® Copyright © 1999, 2000,
2002, 2004 by Holman Bible Publishers. Used by permission.
Scripture quotations marked NIV are taken from the Holy
Bible, New International Version, copyright © 1973, 1978,
1984 by International Bible Society. Scripture quotations
marked NKJV are taken from the New King James Version,
copyright © 1979, 1980, 1982, Thomas Nelson, Inc.,
Publishers. Scripture quotations marked NLT are taken from the
Holy Bible, New Living Translation, copyright © 1996. Used by
permission of Tyndale House Publishers, Inc., Wheaton, Illinois
60189. All rights reserved.

1 2 3 4 5 6 7 8 9 10 09 08 07 06 05

Contents

Preface

If you are familiar with me and know my basic outlook on life, you are probably wondering, *What on earth is Zig going to do with a title like this?* The answer is simple. I'm going to write the book based on conversations with my dog. I chose this format because it gives me the freedom to move in many different directions.

Taffy, our little Welsh Corgi dog, came to live with us early in 1995, a few months before the death of our oldest daughter, Suzan. My daughters Cindy and Julie had collaborated with their mother to bring him into the household through some questionable, though admittedly clever, female strategies. They honestly believed that I would welcome and love him once I saw him. Much to their delight, it took Taffy less than a minute to take control of the entire family—including yours truly. As you can see by his portrait, he is a handsome dog, rich in color, with a heritage that all of us would envy; a personality that wins hearts everywhere; and attitudes that change often enough that anybody's got to like at least one of them.

He is a delight to have around and a marvelous companion for my wife during those times when I'm traveling. He's an extremely personable and entertaining little dog and has brought us many moments of joy. As you will see when you read the book, he also has an awesome sense of humor.

Simple example: My wife Jean, whom I affectionately refer to as "The Redhead" when I'm talking about her, and "Sugar Baby" when I'm talking to her, often tells him that he is a "handsome" dog. It didn't take much to convince him that she was right. Never will I forget the day when I walked down the stairs and noticed that Taffy was lying on the sofa. The Redhead keeps a sheet over it to give him a comfortable place for his frequent naps. We have his portrait on the wall near the sofa, and as I reached the bottom step I noticed that he was looking at the portrait of himself. Looking at it, he would cock his head to the left and then he would cock his head to the right. I asked him, "Dirty Dog, what are you doing?"

He smiled broadly, shifting quickly into a "smug" look and said, "I'm just looking, Dad. You know, I really am a good-looking dog!"

I agreed with him wholeheartedly. Even though I've nicknamed him "Dirty Dog," and I say it with great affection, his royal bloodlines are easy to spot when you look into his regal eyes and stroke his plush coat. I'll explain later how Dirty Dog's nickname came about.

I realized I wanted to make Dirty Dog my coauthor after an event that took place in our backyard. I looked out the back window that brutally hot August day and saw Dirty Dog walking about ten feet behind the neighbor's cat. His tongue was hanging out about as far as it could go, and the cat didn't look much better than he did. Knowing his lack of affection for that particular cat, I called him in and asked him what was going on. In the midst of his panting and laborious breathing he explained that he was chasing that cat and had almost caught him when I called him in. I couldn't believe my ears! "Dirty Dog, you were both walking! What do you mean you were chasing him?"

"Well, Dad, it's so hot—and both of us have fur coats. So we were walking instead of running."

Dirty Dog had a sly little grin on his face when he made that last comment. I don't need to tell you—that broke me up and sealed the coauthor deal.

As you read the book I believe you will discover that Dirty Dog has wide-ranging interests, unusual insights, asks fascinating questions, and sometimes gives startling answers to my questions. Our conversations cover many facets of life, including everything from faith to health, character, relationships, common sense, and any number of other subjects.

I hope you enjoy examining life from Dirty Dog's perspective. I can honestly say that I feel lighter hearted and happier for having done so myself. Now let's get on with the story. Dirty Dog is anxious for me to tell you how all of this came about.

The Genesis

I'll bet you are wondering, "How do you have conversations with a dog, and what on earth would a man and his dog talk about?" Good thought . . . good question.

A number of years ago, my older brother, Preacher Huie Ziglar, who lived in South Alabama, had a dog named Old Bullet. He was a wonderful old dog of mixed heritage, questionable morals, and a penchant for disappearing a day or two at a time. Nevertheless, deep down he had a heart of gold and was loyal to my brother and his family. In his own way he had strong core values, was sensitive, and was a delight to have around. It wasn't until he was in the declining years of his life that I realized Old Bullet was quite a philosopher and carried on some rather extended conversations with my brother. I was privileged to be in on one of them and heard Old Bullet uttering some words of pain and disappointment.

It seems that a stray cat had wandered into the yard and my brother had taken her in, fed her, and made her feel welcome. Old Bullet was out for a walk when the newcomer arrived and was somewhat upset when he returned to discover the new addition. He immediately recognized that he was considerably larger than the cat, and being the gentleman he was he didn't take out his anger and frustration on her but instead went directly to the person who could do something about it. With a mournful face and sadness in his voice Old Bullet said to my brother, "I can't believe you've done this! I've been a faithful dog, a good companion to you and your family. I've protected your interests and run off some big rats and squirrels, not to mention stray dogs that were up to no good. I've never had to go to the vet for anything; I've eaten very little, and most of that was scraps. And yet you take in a complete stranger. Did you really think I would not be upset about this? After all, I've been here several years, and I never once considered going to someone else's place except maybe for a short visit to one of my lady friends, and yet you take in this other animal—and a cat at that! I know it's your place and you don't have to explain, but in light of our relationship I would feel better if you did."

My brother, because of his pastoral background and experience in dealing with disgruntled church members who could be quite cantankerous, had a ready explanation for Old Bullet. He said, "First of all, let me remind you that when I took you in years ago you were skin and bones and weren't much good for anything except eating and sleeping. Yet I never complained or expected much from you except your loyalty and an occasional tail-wagging expression of appreciation. It's true you've been a loyal and good companion, and I believe I've been more than fair with you. I've never raised my hand in anger against you; I've never even really spoken harshly to you except on one occasion when you chased a car and I was afraid you'd get hurt. Not only that, Old Bullet, but to be candid, you have lost a step or two these last two or three years. I even thought I detected signs of loneliness in your countenance during those times when you were lying on the front porch, watching traffic pass without so much as lifting your head. I thought it might be nice for you to have a companion. Actually, this little cat is no threat to you. You'll always be first in my heart and you and I still have some good years together, so let's make our little friend welcome. Who knows . . . you might develop a relationship that will give you much joy and delight. I can tell you this—she'll take the heat off you in the rat-catching department because she can go into smaller places than you can."

With that, Old Bullet was contented, and the case was closed.

That was my introduction to the world of intelligent interchange with animals, so to Old Bullet and my late brother Huie goes much of the credit for this book.

Chapter 1

Communication

Sensitivity Is an Important Part of Communication

On a December day that was cold but still comfortable if you wore a hat and warm clothing, I decided to take "Dirty Dog" (whose official name is "Laffy Taffy" but who responds more readily to "Dirty Dog") for a walk. He was startled when I invited him to go because I hadn't asked him in some little while. His conduct the last time I'd invited him really put me off. Though we'd had many wonderful times on our previous walks, he adamantly refused to go with me that time and no amount of pleading could convince him to join me.

However, this time he was enthusiastic about going, and I've never seen a happier dog when I put his collar and leash on. He was truly excited, and as we started out the door I said, "Dirty Dog, I'm really tickled that you decided to go with me on this one."

He responded, "Well, Dad, I'm glad you asked me. As a matter of fact, I thought you were never going to ask me again."

So I explained to Dirty Dog what the problem was. For the first time in that dog's life he apologized and said he didn't really mean it as a personal affront to me when he refused; it's just that he really wasn't feeling good. Besides, the last time we walked together at Holly Lake I took him too far, kept him out too long, it was too hot and he just about died! He further explained, "You know, Dad, I've got this heavy fur coat and in that hot, humid weather, walking up and down those hills really put a burden on me. It took me two days to get over that! So, the next time you asked me I was just afraid it would be more of the same."

I said, "Well, Dirty Dog, had you told me earlier, we would have shortened that walk and it would not have been so hard on you. In the future I hope you'll keep me better posted." Much to his credit, he promised that he would.

We continued our walk on the street adjoining the golf course, and I could see Dirty Dog scanning the grass and flower beds for stray golf balls. He knows I'm always on the lookout for them, and he takes a lot of pride in the fact that he sniffs them out pretty well himself. When he finds one he always pauses so I can express my deep and sincere appreciation to him. If I don't let him know his golf-ball-finding efforts are appreciated he loses interest in looking, so I learned long ago to praise him for his effort. That's not a bad approach for us to take with our kids and, for that matter, the people we work with. After all, all of us enjoy a little praise and recognition.

When we reached the street on the other side of the golf course the weather was still brisk but not uncomfortable, and I noticed that Dirty Dog's pace was slowing. I asked him what the problem was.

He responded, "Nothing. Everything's all right."

I'll have to inject that I've heard that same response and that same tone of voice from people when they get a little miffed at something and you ask if there is a problem. When they say, "Nothing . . . everything's all right," their tone indicates that everything is far from being all right. To be frank, I was puzzled and didn't know what to say or ask, so I decided I'd wait him out and see if he decided to tell me he would.

After another five minutes or so he interrupted the silence by saying, "Dad, can I tell you something?"

I said, "Certainly, Dirty Dog, what's on your mind?"

He said, "I just want to ask you how much farther are we going to walk?"

I responded, "Why do you ask?"

He said, "Dad, if you'll remember, it's been a long

time since I had a walk and, as you know, I'm mostly trained for sprinting. Running up and down the hall at home chasing my bone which you throw back and forth is good for sprints, but it's not much good for long-distance performance, and I know it's just as far back as it was to get here, so I was just wondering, Dad."

So I said, "Dirty Dog, are you trying to tell me that you would really appreciate it if we turned and headed back home?"

He said, "To be honest, I really would." So we reversed our course and headed for the house.

Actually, he was teaching me a lesson, and I'm glad I caught it. We do need to be sensitive to the feelings of others. Just because I had been walking long distances, there was no way he had been doing that so I acknowledged his physical shortcomings.

At that point he said, "Remember, Dad, I am a Welsh Corgi, and for every step you take on your two long legs I take about eight on my four short ones."

I agreed that not only would we head back in, but I'd slow the pace a little, too. He never said anything else, but he breathed a sigh of relief. The minute he got back to the house he headed for the water, drank enthusiastically for several minutes, and then lay down to take a nap.

The next day was absolutely beautiful. The temperature was about 50 degrees, the sun was shining, there was no wind—an ideal day for a walk. I called out to Dirty Dog to see if he wanted to go. He ignored me. By the time I got the pooper-scooper and his leash I discovered he had disappeared up the stairs. I called him to no avail, explaining what a beautiful day it was and how nice it would be to have a walk. He refused to budge, so I took off and walked by myself.

That evening, after everything had quieted down, I confronted Dirty Dog and asked him what happened and why he was unwilling to do something he so loves to do. He gave me a slight look of *Dad, you just don't get it! Don't you understand?* Though he didn't verbalize it, I knew that was what was on his mind. The look revealed it all. Yes, we do communicate with means other than just verbal expression.

He started to talk and explained by asking a question: "Don't you remember what happened this morning?"

I was puzzled and responded, no, I had no idea what happened.

Then he laid his cards on the table. He said, "Dad, you got up a little before Mom did, and I greeted you with a smile, my bone in my mouth, and a considerable amount of enthusiasm. Now, Dad, you know the signal. I wanted to play. I wanted you to run me up and down the hall, as you always do, but you were busy explaining that you had to review your Sunday school lesson one more time and

9

that you would play later. Well, Dad, that's the time of day I'm at my peak from an energy point of view, and I wanted and needed to play then. But I also noticed, Dad (and this is what really upset me), that you started reading the newspaper. As a matter of fact, you spent a full thirty minutes reading that paper. I was only asking for five minutes . . . that's all, Dad, just five minutes . . . and you know I go at it so hard I'm generally winded and am quite content to call it quits and rest awhile when the five minutes are up."

On reflection I recognized that he was right, that it was thoughtless and inconsiderate for me not to have taken just those five minutes with him. I apologized to Dirty Dog and promised to be more considerate of him in the future. He's generally so accepting of my apologies, but this one seemed to really "bug" him.

So he persisted, explaining, "Dad, you've got to remember what you've been telling people for many years—namely, that 'you can have everything in life you want if you'll just help enough other people get what they want.' Dad, you didn't help me get what I wanted, which was to play and get my wind sprints in. I don't know how you could expect me to give you what you wanted, which was companionship on your walk and in your quest for finding those golf balls. I just hope you're more sensitive to the people in your life and aren't always thinking only of what you want to do because, Dad, it won't work that way. You've got to give before you can expect to get."

Ouch.

Well, I was properly chastised. With a more humble spirit, I promised Dirty Dog that in the future I would be more considerate of meeting his needs and the needs of the people in my life, as well. All in all, it was a winning experience. I learned a lesson, and I felt closer to that little dog than ever before.

Confession Is Good

After a full day of preparing my Sunday school lesson and having lunch and an extended visit with two close friends from church, Dirty Dog and I took off for our walk. However, as is often the case, particularly for the first three or four hundred yards, he had to stop and sniff just about every tree, flower, clump of weeds, mound of grass, or anything in his path, and I constantly admonished him, "Let's go, Dirty Dog, let's go!"

He complained, "Dad, don't be so impatient. What I'm doing is very important."

I asked, "Why so, Dirty Dog?"

He reminded me that dogs stake out their territory. And he said, "You know some dogs are big and bad and others are little like me and have good intentions, but I can tell if it's been five minutes or five hours since one of

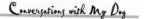

those big bad ones has been along. Dad, I just want to make certain that everything's OK. If I smelled a big, bad one, I would try to guide you in another direction because I'd sure hate for one of them to get hold of you!"

Well, I must admit that I was glad to know Dirty Dog was looking after my best interests. I was a little embarrassed that I had not thought it through a little more carefully myself. So after those first three or four hundred yards, off we went. Since we were headed to the golf course and there were about four houses on the way, would you believe he wanted to take care of a little business in one of those yards? Obviously, since I had not brought along the pooper-scooper I did not permit that. I encouraged him, and we got in a much faster walk until we reached the vacant lot just about fifty yards up the street. I explained to Dirty Dog why we had to speed up.

He replied, "No problem, Dad, everything's going to be OK." And it was.

We did have a nice long walk, but when we got about a half mile from home he again started sniffing around, stopping every fifty feet or so. I kept getting after him to "come on, let's go!" I finally lost my patience with him. I said, "Dirty Dog, I think you're just delaying our return home!"

He kind of grinned and said, "Well, Dad, to be honest, I wasn't in quite as good shape as I thought. You know, we haven't been walking very much the last two months. Frankly, I just overdid it so I was kind of killing time until I got my breath."

I have to tell you I appreciated his honesty, and I believe there is a lesson there that will benefit all of us. When you've been caught in a deal like that, you need to be honest enough to confess it and confront the issues. I think even more of Dirty Dog because he 'fessed up that he was stalling so he could catch his breath. And now that I know what the problem was, I'll be more understanding in the future. I believe when we deal with dogs and/or people, if we will try to understand why they do certain things, it will help us get along lots better with them.

He'd Been Thinking

I was reading quietly in the den when I noticed that Dirty Dog was standing right in front of me, not saying anything but just looking. I asked him what was on his mind.

He responded, "Dad, I want to talk to you about a joke you've been telling that gets a good laugh out of everybody who hears it. As a matter of fact, Dad, you get so tickled before you deliver the punch line that you start laughing yourself—which, incidentally, I've always seen as kind of strange. But that's your business, and since you seem to enjoy it I figure it is all right for you to indulge yourself."

I thanked him for his understanding and asked him which joke he was referring to.

He said, "You know, Dad, the one you tell about the fellow who tied his huge German Shepherd to a post just outside a bar and went inside to have a drink. First of all, Dad, I know you don't approve of drinking, so I'm surprised you tell that joke. Then you point out that after the man had been in the bar a half hour or so a timid little man came in. Since there was only one patron at the bar he went straight to him and said, 'Mister, was that your big German Shepherd outside?' The man acknowledged that it was. The timid little man apologetically explained, 'Well, I want to apologize to you because my dog just killed your dog.' The bar patron was startled and said, 'What kind of dog do you have?' The response from the little fellow was, 'A Chihuahua.' The patron was stunned. He said, 'What? A Chihuahua killed my German Shepherd? How on earth did he do it?' And the timid little man said, 'He choked your dog to death when he was trying to swallow him.'

"Well, Dad, I guess you people think that's funny, but let's look at it from a dog's perspective. That German Shepherd undoubtedly had a mom and a dad and who knows how many brothers and sisters. Think about how they feel that they've just lost a blood relative. For that matter, Dad, I suspect that the owner of that big German Shepherd loved him. You keep telling me, Dad, that you love me, so it's just natural that I'm going to believe the owner of the German Shepherd loved him."

I tried to explain to Dirty Dog that it was just a joke, and that in all probability it never really happened.

Dirty Dog's response to that was, "Well, Dad, that's the problem. Just like I've heard you say about television, although most of what you're seeing is fiction, a lot of people act it out in real life. The authorities maintain that watching murders, fights, drunken brawls, stabbings, etc., on television plays a role in violence in everyday life. As a matter of fact, Dad, I've heard you give a number of specific examples which closely link violence on television to violence in real life. So I'm just afraid that some of you people—or, for that matter, some big dogs—might take it out on other little dogs because they'll be more careful and not try to swallow the little ones, but just chew 'em up and spit 'em out. I'm really concerned, Dad."

Well, Dirty Dog had a point—and he pursued it with another thought. "Suppose, Dad, that a 360-pound lineman in the National Football League got upset with a small wide receiver and tried to swallow him. Would you think that was funny?"

I tried to explain to Dirty Dog that was highly unlikely, that people just don't do things like that. And then I'll have to confess I closed out on this conversation as a loser, because Dirty Dog simply said, "Dad, you haven't been watching any of that television that you say those unkind things about as far as violence is concerned. Sometimes when I'm bored during the day when you and Mom leave me, I watch that sort of stuff. I'm telling you that what people do to one another is a whole lot worse than what dogs do to other dogs."

I had no answer for that one, and I was relieved when Dirty Dog let the subject drop.

Disappointment

One evening Dirty Dog just walked into my office and lay down at my feet. I was busy putting the finishing touches on a book, but I felt that I needed to pause for a moment or two and listen to what he had to say.

It doesn't happen often, but on this occasion he was quite apologetic. Earlier that afternoon when I had gotten ready for my walk he ignored me. Five hours had passed and Dirty Dog was mumbling a little bit, seeming to be uncertain about how to say what he obviously felt he must say. Finally, he got started. His opening comment said a lot.

"You know, Dad, there's a reason I didn't want to walk with you earlier today. I had heard you on the phone saying you were headed for a really good one, and that always means you are going to be walking far and fast. I don't always mind that, Dad, except on those walks you are so intent on a brisk walk that you seldom take time to either talk or listen to what I might have to say. And, frankly, I just wasn't in any mood for that kind of treatment today. However, when you and Mom went out to dinner, I had over an hour alone to think, and I realized that I had disappointed you. I could tell by the look on your face. And, Dad, I really didn't want to disappoint you. Surely you know by now that most of the time I really enjoy our walks, but today somehow I just didn't feel in the mood. Oh, I admit I regret it now, but it's just one of those things, Dad. Maybe tomorrow, if you'll ask me again, we can have a really good make-up walk."

Since Dirty Dog explained himself so well and so sincerely, I assured him that all was well and we would have our make-up walk the very next day. He smiled.

Some Walks Are Better Than Others

Dirty Dog was fairly quiet as we returned from our walk the next day. To get the conversation ball rolling I asked him why he'd refused to walk with me the last time I'd asked him.

He said, "Just because."

When I pressed him for more information he really let it out.

"Dad, you've got to understand that dogs are just like people in many ways. We don't always have a reason why we do or don't do something, and I don't know, I guess I just didn't want to. I had no real reason. I didn't feel bad; I didn't think I had been mistreated or abused in any way. You, and especially Mom, had been loving and kind to me in every way. I just didn't want to go. And, Dad, I hope you can have some empathy and understand that sometimes that's just the way it is. You seem to be able to do that with people. I'm having trouble believing that you're prejudiced, Dad, that you would show discrimination after all those speeches you make about how you hate prejudice, how you think it's so terribly wrong for people to discriminate."

I wasn't going to challenge him on his point so I asked him why he so willingly went along with me on the walk today.

He said, and I quote him directly: "Dad, don't you remember that before you went up to take your nap you told Mom that you were going to take a walk later?"

I admitted that I did.

He said, "Well, I knew that since you were going to take a nap first, that meant you would not be in any kind of hurry. I just hate it, Dad, when I feel rushed on these walks and you feel like you've got to go a mile a minute because Dr. Cooper says you've got to walk fast in order to get in better condition. Well, that's fine for you, Dad, but as I've heard you say, 'Dirty Dog is a full-size dog with pint-size legs.' Dad, I just can't cover as much ground—unless I'm running—as you can. When you came downstairs after your nap I could see that you were in no hurry. As a matter of fact, you took a minute or two to pet me and talk to me and roll me on my back on the floor and tickle my tummy and even spin me around a couple of times. Incidentally, Dad, I like to do a little of that, but sometimes you overdo it! Anyway, I figured you were not in a hurry so I was delighted to go for the walk."

Then I said, "Dirty Dog, I know you sniff around so you can protect me from bad dogs, but why is it that when we first start our walk you have to stop a dozen times (it seems like) before you finally get into gear?"

And again he explained to me, "Well, Dad, you know, dogs have certain business they have to take care of that you people don't know anything about. For example, Dad, you're nearly five feet taller than I am. I'm built low to the ground. Now that gives you some advantages, but it gives me some advantages, too. When I pause and sniff and, I'll admit, frequently raise my leg for you-know-what, I'm really just 'marking the territory.' I let these neighborhood dogs—most of whom I know and get along well with, but some I don't—know that I've been by and that I'm reclaiming the territory as my own. That's what I'm doing, Dad. I know you've read the book *Territorial Prerogative* and recognize the importance for both dogs and people to have territories of their own.

"If you'll remember that in your dealing with people, it'll help you get along better with 'em, Dad. Not only that, but you'll be a better teacher and you can help more folks in their 'human relations,' and help them to win more friends and influence more people."

Well, I thought the conversation was over, but Dirty Dog really was "wound up" and spitting out good information and advice, so I ventured another question: "Well, Dirty Dog, do you have anything you'd like to volunteer that I should know and be aware of?"

"Well," he said, "now that you mention it, Dad, I really do. I know that you're a 'high I and a high D,' and I've heard you talking about those characteristics of the various personalities from the 'DISC' program. I know that you're kind of impetuous, that you want to 'run the show,' you want to be in control, but at the same time it also tells me that you want to get along well with people and have them like you. So for your information, Dad, the same qualities are present in us dogs. I'm more like Mom in that respect, Dad. As you know, she's a 'low I, low D,' but 'high S and high C.' She's more curious—that's the way I am. I like to look into things. She's more patient and she's not nearly as impetuous as you—that's the way I am, Dad. I don't just like to 'go there to get there.' I like to be learning things on the way. And you know Mom's the same way, and you certainly seem to understand and get along with her. Dad, you've got to remember the 'type' of person or dog you're dealing with and be considerate of his personality needs. For instance, if you'll be more patient with me, I'll try harder to understand when necessity forces you to be in a hurry and you really don't have time to play or even talk to me."

Dirty Dog certainly gave me a thorough short course in communication and human/dog nature. If I can consistently communicate the way he has suggested I should, life's road will be much smoother.

Chapter 2

Three H's—
Dog Hair, Hugs, and Humor

I'm Not a Back Seat Dog, Dad!

Virtually everyone who knows me is going to be stunned—particularly if they've not seen me the last couple of years—to know that I've developed such an affection for my little dog. For years I had vigorously protested there would be no more pets in my house. However, when the Redhead and our daughters went to the dog show and saw little Welsh Corgis which, incidentally, are the breed Queen Elizabeth has, they fell in love with them. The Redhead really wanted one because I am gone a great deal and she felt a dog would be a lot of company. Getting Dirty Dog was an incredibly good decision. He has been a delightful companion when I take my walks and lots of company for the Redhead when I'm gone.

Another Front-Seat Driver

I'll never forget the first time I took him on a car ride. I put him in the back seat, and he loudly and in no uncertain terms displayed his displeasure right away. I told him just to keep quiet and enjoy the ride or I'd take him back home. When we returned he said, "Dad, I didn't mean to upset you, but I just felt like I was in the wrong place. I'm just not a back-seat dog. You might remember that I come from a royal line. Remember, Queen Elizabeth has Welsh Corgis. If you'll just look at hers and look at me, I think you'll agree we are from the same family. But I'm better-looking, healthier, more active, and a lot more fun than any of her dogs are, so my proper place is in the front seat."

Well, he was pretty persuasive, and I started to see things from his perspective. I was glad Dirty Dog's self-image was good enough that he could protest when he felt that he'd been unfairly treated or was not being given the proper respect. It didn't really take any extra time to listen to his views, and it gave him a feeling of importance. After all, he had a point when he said, "You know, Dad, if I'm going to shed any hairs they'll come off in the back seat as well as the front, and they'll be no more difficult to remove from the front than they will from the back. Besides, I can see better, and since you've gotten a little hard of hearing it is just more fitting that you and I sit closer together. That way I'll only have to shout half as loud when we visit and catch up on things." Dirty Dog had a really good point.

Keep the Love Light Burning

On one of our visits to "Sugarville," Dirty Dog and I had a serious conversation while his mother took a little siesta. We walked down to the pier behind our lake house, and Dirty Dog broke the silence first.

He said, "Well, Dad, I was just thinking. Many of my friends tell me that in the homes where they live they notice that husbands and wives seem to tolerate each other instead of enjoy each other. But you and Mom seem to have so much fun together. Every time I look up you're hugging her. I'm just wondering why there is such a difference."

My response was very simple. "Well, Dirty Dog, I'm sure you've heard me tell others that your mother is affectionately known as 'The Happy Hugger.' That if anything is moving she'll stop it and hug it, and if it's not moving she'll dust it off and sell it. So yes, Dirty Dog, suspect we'll hug fifteen, twenty, maybe even thirty times a day. Now, they're not long hugs, Dirty Dog, and they're not sensual, but what those hugs really say is, 'I love you and I enjoy being with you.' And since she hugs so freely and enjoys it so much, and quite obviously I do, we just take advantage of every opportunity to get a hug!"

He said, "Well, I've noticed that, Dad, but I've often wondered why it is that when you come into the house you hug Mom and when you leave the house you hug her; when she walks by your office upstairs you get up from behind the desk and go hug her again. While I think that's neat, aren't you overdoing it, Dad?"

"Dirty Dog, you can never overdo sharing your love and affection for your mate. That's one of the reasons after fifty-eight years your mom and I are more in love than ever, have more fun than ever, talk more, and 'hang out' more than ever. We just enjoy each other's company."

"Well, don't misunderstand, Dad, I'm glad you do, but I was just wondering. It seems to me that other folks would do the same thing."

"Well, I've often wondered why they don't myself. Maybe they were raised in non-hugging families and for whatever reason they've never broken the cycle—which is really easy to do. Hugging is not a difficult thing to do and doesn't require a lot of skill. Actually, the more you do it the better you get at it and the more you enjoy it. The more love you show, the more love you feel. Love without demonstration is hard to identify, Dirty Dog, so never withhold hugs, tail wags, smiles, or any other outward sign that you're delighted to see and be with someone. As a Jewish scholar wrote thousands of years ago, 'Love is patient and kind. Love is not jealous or boastful or proud or rude. Love does not demand its own way. Love is not irritable, and it keeps no record of when it has been wronged. It is never glad about injustice but rejoices whenever the truth wins out. Love never gives up, never loses faith, is always hopeful, and endures through every circumstance'" (1 Cor. 13:4–7 NLT).

Actually, as a result of the conversation Dirty Dog was almost in a daze. As we walked back up to the house he said, "You know, Dad, that's a pretty heavy load you just put on me, but I'm glad you did because it does help explain why you and Mom love each other so much and why Tom, Cindy, and Julie always love being around this home, because it is filled with love. Thank you for sharing that with me, Dad."

Yup. Dirty Dog was glad I had let him in on what was happening. I'll bet your kids will be, too, if you'll let them know why and how you keep the love light burning in your home.

Even though Dirty Dog had an early trip to the veterinarian and will never have a dog family of his own, he's probably the most family-oriented member in our household. His questions indicate that is at least partially true. For instance, the very next day I was reading the newspaper when Dirty Dog pawed my leg and asked, "Dad, why do you think you and Mom love each other more today than ever before in your fifty-eight years of marriage? Is it because of all of those hugs?"

That was a good question, and I believe every husband and wife will be interested in knowing the answer. So I said, "Well, Dirty Dog, there are several reasons, and the hugs are partially responsible. First, we have disagreed on many occasions, and still do, but we've never gotten so angry that we said mean, nasty, ugly things to each other. We've never called each other unkind names, never accused each other of being 'dumb' or 'stupid,' or claimed 'that was an idiotic thing to say or do!' The message is that because we do love and respect each other, we just don't say or do things like that."

Dirty Dog replied, "Well, that certainly makes it easier to forgive and make up when the little tiffs are settled, doesn't it?"

I said, "Exactly! We've not allowed our disagreement to build a wall between us. We always leave the door wide open so that we can get back in each other's good graces with a minimum of difficulty. That's the way we eliminated much of the negative, but let's look at the positive things that really make a difference.

"We each, for many years, have considered the wants and needs of the other, and as a wise man once said, a successful marriage requires two things: A giver and a forgiver. So each of us has always forgiven the other. When an apology is made and forgiveness is asked, then it's all over, Dirty Dog. We don't bring it back up; it's a done deal."

Dirty Dog was casually impressed with that and said it was a great idea. However, I was not through with the subject, so I pointed out that at every opportunity the Redhead and I look for things to do for each other that the other is capable of doing for himself or herself.

He asked why I put in the part about "the other is capable of doing for himself or herself."

I explained, "Well, Dirty Dog, if she can't do it for herself, then it becomes a duty or a responsibility for me to do it for her. While a responsibility is important, and all husbands and wives should accept their responsibility, that doesn't really breed romance. As you know, your mom and I are strong believers in romance."

He said, "Yes, I've observed that, Dad, a few thousand times since I've been in this home. I've been listening when you thought I was snoozing and, of course, when my eyes are wide open I can both see and hear what's going on. I notice those little things, Dad, and to be honest, I believe that if everybody did them, there would be lots more really happy marriages instead of just marriages."

Everybody Enjoys a Laugh

When Dirty Dog came strutting into my office I could tell he was in a great frame of mind, so I asked him what he was so happy about. He explained that he had been listening in when Mom was on the telephone. Since she laughed so much it had gotten him tickled and made him feel really good all over.

"Well," I commented, "that's what makes me feel good all over, too."

He said, "Dad, I heard, according to what people say at Bible study, that you tell jokes before you even start teaching your Sunday school lesson at church on Sundays."

I told him that he'd heard right. I responded that we Christians have more to laugh about than anybody, and that certainly in God's house it made sense that people who might have had a tough week would appreciate a laugh or two.

He said, "Well, apparently they do because they sure talk about it a lot!"

Then he wanted me to give him some examples of how I got them laughing and why I feel humor is so important. I told him about the little boy who was told by his mother to get the fly swatter and see if he could eliminate the flies that were trapped on the enclosed porch. In a few minutes he came back reporting that he had killed five of them, two boys and three girls. His mother was somewhat stunned and asked, "How on earth could you tell the difference?" He answered, "It was easy. The two boys were on the beer cans and the three girls were on the telephone."

Well, I'll have to admit that Dirty Dog didn't break out in laughter at that one, so I decided to give him two more examples and read from some church bulletins: "The peace-making meeting scheduled for today has been canceled due to a conflict," and "Barbara remains in the hospital and needs blood donors for more transfusions. She is also having trouble sleeping and requests tapes of our pastor's sermons." One more, "Don't let worry kill you off—let the church help."

Then I decided to throw in a couple of comments from court records:

Question: She had three children, right?

Answer: Yes.

Question: "How many were boys?"

Answer: None.

Question: "Were there any girls?"

What is your date of birth? "July 15." What year? "Every year."

The trouble with some women is that they get all excited about nothing and then marry it.

Then I decided to explain to Dirty Dog that a sense of humor has huge benefits. For example, in any organization, everything else being equal, people are generally recognized and rewarded if they are pleasant, easy to get along with, and have a sense of humor that is punctuated with laughter. I also told him there are some specific physical benefits to enjoying a good sense of humor. For example, research shows that school students and people who use humor as a coping mechanism were more likely to be optimistic and positive than those who did not have a sense of humor. They also know that people with a strong sense of humor are far less likely to become depressed about life.

Research also shows that your blood pressure and your heart rate are affected by a sense of humor. It enables you to relax and, according to doctors, laughter is internal jogging, which, in essence, stimulates endorphins, which are the brain's natural pain-killers. And, of course, there are many who contend that humor and creativity are closely related.

I explained to him that his mom and I laugh together a great deal, and he slipped in the comment that he had noticed that. He even admitted that he enjoyed hearing us laugh because it means that we are getting along well, having fun, and in short, it makes things around the house a whole lot better.

Then I explained to Dirty Dog that it's economical to laugh. Needless to say, this puzzled him and he asked for an explanation. I pointed out that if you have a tendency to laugh and suppress the laughter, the laughter reverses itself, comes back inside, and spreads your hips. Well, I'm not certain he quite got the gist of what I was saying, but I couldn't help but laugh myself as I told it, and that amused him. "As a matter of fact, people often tell me, Dirty Dog, that they enjoy listening to my jokes because I get so tickled myself when I'm telling them. Sometimes some of them are so funny, Dirty Dog, I just can't help it! I have fun laughing.

"And here's one of those interesting things about life: People who have a sense of humor and an easy, ready laugh are always nice to be around. As a general rule, they end up with more friends than those who don't have a good sense of humor."

Next Dirty Dog wanted to know what kind of jokes I tell. In an effort to teach him some important lessons in life, I explained that first of all I never tell any sexist or racist jokes. And I never tell jokes that involve any kind of profanity or language that a parent would not want his seven-year-old to hear. Those kinds of jokes don't win friends and influence people; they lose friends and alienate many others. All in all, it was a pretty interesting conversation. At the end of it, Dirty Dog acknowledged that he was glad he lived in a home were there was a lot of good, fun-loving laughter going on.

It matters not if the topic is dog hair, hugs and love, or even humor; every conversation I have with Dirty Dog deepens our relationship. Visit with the ones you love and remember that those who laugh together—stay together.

Chapter 3

Consideration

Be Thoughtful of Others

Dirty Dog was waiting at the bottom of the stairs. The look in his eyes told me he was excited about going on another walk with me. I put his collar and leash on. As we passed through the front door he said, "Dad, could we take a different route this time? I get tired of going the same way all the time."

I reflected on what he said and realized that sometimes we get so accustomed to doing what we want to do we overlook the possibility that perhaps our mate, child, associate or even a "Dirty Dog" might prefer a different option. I immediately agreed that we would take the "scenic route" this time. Since we would be walking through a neighborhood, I went to get the pooper-scooper.

We'd gone only a few steps when Dirty Dog said, "You know, Dad, I appreciate your willingness to take a different route, and I'm glad you brought the pooper-scooper because I have a feeling it's going to come in handy on this trip." Then he elaborated and said, "You know, Dad, I notice that many of our neighbors walk their dogs, but I almost never see one of them carrying a pooper-scooper. That's too bad because from my vantage point at the window, I see them pause in our front yard and since I'm a dog myself, I know exactly what they're up to. I'm certain our neighbors would never dream of stopping by and dumping their garbage, or throwing their trash on our lawn, and yet they let their dogs do their business in our front yard. It really isn't very thoughtful or neighborly is it, Dad?"

I had to agree that Dirty Dog was right on this issue. I figured he was through with the subject, but he had much more to say.

"You know, Dad, I'm glad you have that pooper-scooper because, truth is, these other pet owners put their dogs in precarious positions and give them bad reputations when really all they're doing is what comes naturally. The owners are the responsible parties. I'm glad you're looking after my best interests because I'd hate for the neighbors to get upset when they saw that we were not prepared to handle emergencies which do frequently occur on our walks."

I give Dirty Dog credit for a lot of insight on that particular observation. When we had circled the first block and headed for the street that leads to walking around the lake, the conversation lightened a little. Dirty Dog commented that the view was certainly "better over here."

He was just hoping something exciting would happen, like maybe an opportunity to chase one of the ducks that frequent the lake and sometimes walk out on the paths. As it developed that didn't happen, but he was content just to walk casually along, eyeballing whatever happened to come into view and feeling very important as a result of having gotten his way on the trip we were taking.

Be Considerate

It was a beautiful day, and as I headed downstairs I invited Dirty Dog to go on my walk with me. He was lying on about the fourth step of the stairs, and I told him I'd run back and get his collar and leash and we'd be off. It took a matter of twenty seconds, but when I returned Dirty Dog was nowhere to be found. He had scooted upstairs. When I encouraged him to come on down he reappeared at the top of the stairs, lay down, and just looked at me.

Well, I was truly disappointed, but I started my walk without him. The temperature was perfect, the sun was shining, and I had a chance to chat a moment with some golfers who were passing by. When I returned home, after a time Dirty Dog came strolling in and asked a big question: "Dad, could I talk with you for a moment?"

And I said, "Why, certainly, Dirty Dog, what have you got on your mind?"

He said, "Well, I need in all fairness to explain something to you because I believe it will help our relationship and improve communication in the future. I distinctly heard Mom when she told you that I was not feeling well, that I had gotten sick to my stomach, and some green stuff had come up. Now, Dad, I didn't know what the green stuff was; all I know is that I was feeling really lousy. My energy bucket was empty (I've heard you use those very words, Dad), and I just simply did not want to go for a walk.

"I know you were disappointed, Dad, but perhaps out of it something good will come. I know how sensitive you are to Mom, but Dad, you also need to be sensitive to me. After Mom and Betty Jean (our housekeeper of thirty-plus years) told you I had been sick, I'm surprised you didn't comfort me a little, talk to me quietly and say if I wanted to go for a walk you'd be willing to walk at a more casual pace. But no, that never entered the picture. You were disappointed and I think I detected just a slight bit of irritation, maybe even a little anger in your voice when I didn't respond the way you expected me to. Dad, I just didn't need that at the time. I'm not trying to 'Corgi' you—and don't look so surprised at that statement. As you know, I'm from royal lines, and I just think that sounds a whole lot better than 'I don't want to hound you.' In a way, Dad, it's pretty sad that this derogatory statement even exists.

Thanks to uncaring, insensitive people, the things they've said about hounds makes a person think hounds are not worthy of proper respect and praise. There was even one fellow who sang a song with the line, 'You Ain't Nothin' but a Hound Dog!'

"From my perspective I believe that's one of the reasons some hounds look sad on a fairly regular basis. Think about it, Dad. If somebody used similar words about you, you know how that would make you feel. The point I want to get across is that I don't want to badger you—oh, boy, I did it again, didn't I?—because the badger is a very fine, tough little critter that stands up for his rights and is a fierce fighter when his territory is challenged. But all I'm trying to say is I want to continue your education, Dad, in making you more sensitive to me—and to others as well.

"Part of what I'm trying to accomplish is to reiterate (bet you didn't know I knew that word, did you?) what I've said before and I've heard you say, that we do pass attitudes on. For example, when somebody says or does something nice to you or for you, I know it puts you in a great frame of mind, and then you treat other people even nicer. On those rare occasions when you've taken me to your office and we stop to read some of the new letters that have been posted, I've noticed how excited you get when somebody says something nice about you.

"Just before your walk I heard you talking to a fellow on the telephone. Judging from the drift of the conversation, he had listened to an audiotape about your 'Spiritual Journey' and, as a result, had become a Christian. I heard you say that was the best news you could ever receive. Well, I like to receive good news, too, because you see, Dad, the way you treat me determines to a very large degree how I'm going to treat the people who come visit us in our home. I've noticed the better you treat Mom, the better she treats me, so, Dad, I'm actually trying to get you to treat everybody like they really ought to be treated. No, I'm not lecturing you. I'm just giving you some of the same information I've heard you give to other people."

Well, when Dirty Dog finally ran down, I was properly chastised. I might have gone too far in my apology and my promise that in the future not only would I be more sensitive, but I would even go out of my way to treat him like the royalty he is. It seemed that I owed him as much after my talk about being considerate enough to carry a pooper-scooper and then not even being thoughtful enough to consider the fact that he wasn't feeling well but thought only about myself and my desire for company on my walk.

Chapter 4

Trust, Traditions, and Resolutions

Our Protector and Us Fellas

One morning as Dirty Dog returned to the living room window after one of his many explosive trips to the backyard gate, I asked him why, when he sees people walk by on the sidewalk, he feels compelled to run through the dog door and bark at those people. He explained to me that he was just establishing the fact that in the event they were walking for the wrong reason—namely to spot out likely targets for later breaking into—his house is under the watchcare of a very effective alarm system as well as a guard dog who would defend his home at all costs. Though it does require considerable effort to make the countless trips back and forth, he explained that we never know what some people's motives might be. As the official "alarm system" for the Ziglar household, he needed to warn any potential predators that this was the last house in town they would want to invade.

I was thinking about how Dirty Dog rushes around to protect our home, and I was reminded of another time Dirty Dog got in a hurry. So I asked him, "Dirty Dog, every morning when we get up and you hear me unlock the front door, you come tearing down the stairs like you are escaping a fire! What's going on?"

Dirty Dog responded, "Well, Dad, I've heard you talk about habits from time to time and the fact that our lives represent a long series of habits. You develop good habits, and over a period of time things will become automatic, and you'll have a successful as well as a balanced life. If you develop bad habits, you will have a long series of bad experiences, and life will continue to be a challenge, a puzzle, and a frustration. Actually, Dad, I've noticed that when you get up in the morning you get busy. So when I hear the door open I know that you're up and about to get busy. You know, Dad, I like to follow good examples, so I hustle down those stairs. While you're getting the newspaper I take care of the first issue of the day and then I'm ready for a little action. Actually, it's one of the few things 'us fellas' do together regularly when you're home, Dad. I've noticed that when you play golf you generally play with Tom, and I think that's neat. But I want a special occasion, too, Dad, where it is just the two of us, so we can have that 'bonding' like you and Tom have. That's the real reason I rush down those steps, Dad."

To be candid, I thought that showed unusual insight on Dirty Dog's part. I complimented him for it because I felt that he was teaching and reinforcing things I had believed for a long time and, more important, things that our readers would respond to and perhaps duplicate.

*T*rust

Dirty Dog sauntered into my office and said, "I have a couple of things on my mind, Dad. I've noticed that you talk about parables and trust an awful lot. What is a parable, Dad?"

I explained to him that a parable is a little story with a big message.

Naturally, that aroused his curiosity and he said, "Give me an example."

I said, "OK, Dirty Dog. This parable involves characters named Fire, Water, and Trust. The three of them were walking through a village that bordered on deep woods. They asked a native about the deep woods and were assured that they were deep and very dark. Then they made a request, 'In case we get lost and are not back by tomorrow, would you send someone in to look for us?' The villager said, 'Well, in the case of fire, that will be easy because where there is fire there is smoke. As far as finding water, that's easy because when we see something green and growing we know water is around. But I encourage you to keep your eye on trust, because once trust is lost, it's very difficult to find.'"

Then I decided to elaborate. I explained to Dirty Dog that Francis Fukuyama, a Japanese educator and author, in his book *Trust: The Social Virtues and the Creation of Prosperity,* points out that after studying several cultures and generations he was able to trace the growth and success of a society by the level of trust in that society. Trust, I told Dirty Dog, is the key to building winning relationships at home, on the job, and in government.

"There are even some people, Dirty Dog, who say that character isn't really that important, that what happens in your personal life has no bearing on what you do in your public life, and that things are 'relative.' That simply is not true, Dirty Dog. No business person would hire a treasurer or CPA who admitted that he or she was only 'relatively honest.' Certainly when it comes to being 'relative,' your mom has never asked me, not even one time, after I returned from an out-of-town trip if I had been 'relatively faithful' to her. I'll even guarantee you, Dirty Dog, that she is not going to ask that question. Some things are right; some things are wrong. And character does count because it generates trust if consistently practiced or mistrust if character falters.

"And as an aside, Dirty Dog, I want you to know that my observation of you is that you are very consistent and have impeccable character. That's one of the reasons I chose you as the coauthor of this book. I knew I could trust you, Dirty Dog."

Well, as I looked at Dirty Dog he truly had "happy eyes" that fairly sparkled with joy. Yes, all of us like to have nice things said about us, don't we?

The Christmas Season

It was a special day at our house. The hour of our company Christmas party was fast approaching, and the Redhead had spent countless hours decorating the Christmas trees and making certain everything was in order. I contributed by doing the physical tasks of bringing in and setting up extra chairs and tables.

Dirty Dog was watching all of this activity with intense interest, and his curiosity finally got the best of him. He asked what was going on. We explained that we decided to make the company Christmas party a little more personal this year by having it in our home, so we were having the meal catered and all the employees and their guests would be arriving soon. We planned to sing Christmas carols, I would read the Christmas story, and then we would exchange socks. Dirty Dog looked at me with disbelief until I explained that we had drawn names for the gift exchange and had agreed that the gifts would be Christmas socks.

Dirty Dog exclaimed, "That's a great idea, Dad. I've got to tell you that some of those Christmas socks are really sharp-looking, some are wild-looking, but it seems to me that some go beyond the realm of good taste."

It was obvious that Dirty Dog was excited when the Redhead put his Christmas kerchief and ribbon on him. He looked all decked out, and his eyes seemed to dance as he eagerly anticipated the arrival of the guests. He is truly a "people" dog (actually, he thinks he's a person).

Dirty Dog's relationship with people he does not know is a peculiar one. He barks heartily at newcomers, giving the impression that he might be one vicious little dog, but then he goes up and licks them. I'm afraid he wouldn't be much help as a watchdog. As a matter of fact, he would probably lead a burglar right to where the "goodies" are hidden! Anyhow, he received a lot of attention as everyone arrived, and he personally greeted them, calling some of them by name since many of our folks visit us regularly. The music was beautiful, and though he made no effort to join in, it was obvious he enjoyed the festivities. He was a little puzzled that no one offered him even a taste of the Christmas goodies, but he was content with the bone he received as a gift and relieved that he hadn't received silly Christmas socks.

The highlight of the evening came when the employees of our company presented the Redhead and me with a special Christmas present—and it was special. It was the beautiful portrait of Dirty Dog that I mentioned in the preface of this book.

The portrait came about in a most interesting way. Every Friday the Redhead goes to the beauty shop, and on one particular Friday I was out of town. Our daughter, Cindy, came by and "kidnapped" Dirty Dog, took him to the portrait studio where King Harrell, the photographer for many of our family and company events, spent two hours trying to get Dirty Dog to assume his best regal portrait pose. The results were absolutely magnificent, and it's one of the neatest and most treasured gifts we've ever received. As I said, we have it proudly and prominently displayed in our living room.

New Year's Resolutions

With Christmas behind us New Year's day dawned, and Dirty Dog and I were the first two awake and up. It was nice and cold outside, so we built a cozy, warm fire, and we were very comfortably seated before it when Dirty Dog asked me what all the excitement was about.

I explained that we, along with Richard and Cindy and his buddy, Emmit, were on our annual trip to "Sugarville" to celebrate Cindy's birthday, December 31.

We have a tradition of spending several days together, overdosing on football games, long walks, lengthy conversations, lots of food, and just relaxing and preparing for the new year.

Then Dirty Dog said, "Well, Dad, I keep hearing people talk about 'Happy New Year' and 'New Year's resolutions,' and things like that. What do they mean by 'New Year's resolutions'?"

I said, "Well, Dirty Dog, for a long time people have been making what they call New Year's resolutions, saying, 'At the first of the year I'm going to get on a diet and lose twenty-one pounds,' or 'Beginning the first of the year I'll get on an exercise program and do something about this expanding waistline,' or 'I'm going to start reading good books more every day,' etc. The reality is that New Year's resolutions have fallen under a great deal of criticism because so many people make them on the spur of the moment, without giving them any really serious thought, so they rarely follow through."

Then I said to Dirty Dog, "And that's too bad, because New Year's resolutions might be the most important thing we do if we clearly understand the way to make and follow through on those resolutions." He wanted to know more, so I explained to him: "First of all, Dirty Dog, when you make a resolution what you need to do next is repeat the resolution to people who will hold you accountable. For example, your mate, your employer, your sales manager, your physician, people like that who have an interest in your well-being. The best way to do this is to repeat the resolution many times, not only in front of one person but in front of several people: 'This is what I am going to do beginning January 1.' Now, actually, Dirty Dog, we can make resolutions at any time of the year. The only thing I don't like about resolutions is that a lot of people think they've got to wait until January 1 to make them. But here's the major point: If they make that New Year's resolution and then repeat it a number of times in front of people who will hold them accountable, the first thing you know, one day they will have said it enough times that they will verbally stomp their feet and say, 'I'm going to do it!' Now the resolution has moved to the decision stage.

"Once that decision is made, Dirty Dog, any thinking person (and this is the way the mind works—it moves forward step by step by step) who makes the decision, *I am going to do this,* his or her next thought in the mental process is, *Well, I've got to have a plan of action in order for this to happen,* so then they lay out the plan of action in order to accomplish their objective. Then they list the benefits that will be theirs by reaching the goal they are setting. You see, Dirty Dog, a lot of times people will make a resolution like 'I'm going to stop drinking' or 'I'm going to stop smoking,' then their next thought is, *Oh, but if I stop smoking I know I'll gain weight!* In other words, they concentrate on the negative. So the first thing we want to do is concentrate on the positive: 'If I reach this goal I'll feel better, I'll look better, I'll smell better, I'll have more energy,' I mean things like that, Dirty Dog.

"Then once they've identified all of the benefits, the next step they need to take is to look at the obstacles they've got to overcome. If they had no obstacles, Dirty Dog, they already would have done what they need to do. Obstacles might be things like lack of discipline, not having the ability to stick to what they want to do, and other things. Just what are the obstacles? Maybe they need a new car to reach their goal. Maybe they need to have a better education to accomplish their objective. Whatever it is that stands in the way, they need to make a list of them.

"Next, they need to list the skills and knowledge they need to acquire to reach their goal. Then they need to make a list of the people, the groups, and the organizations they need to work with to reach their goal. And finally, they commit all of this to paper in the form of a specific plan—step one, step two, step three, etc. They establish the date they plan to reach the goal and immediately start and follow through.

"It's amazing what that will do! Research shows that if they put all of this in writing they are over three times as likely to reach their objectives as people who do not put it in writing. So, Dirty Dog, I hope all of our readers will take seriously what this book is all about, and what New Year's resolutions are all about, and that they will follow through. Because if they do, Dirty Dog, then they will live fuller, happier, richer, more prosperous, productive, better-balanced lives. After all, isn't that what we all want, Dirty Dog? I believe it is. And I believe our readers will agree with that."

Chapter 5

Discipline

*P*arental Guidance and Laws

"Well, Dirty Dog, you did it again! I invited you to go for a walk with me. You originally accepted, then started backing away and moving in your mother's direction. However, past experience told me you were just being a little coy, so I put the chain and collar on you and off we went. As usual, you bit at the chain and acted contrary for a few yards and then away you went! We did have a great walk.

"The thing I want to know, Dirty Dog, is why do you rebel almost every time before we take our walk?"

"Well, Dad, I didn't think I'd ever have to tell you this because I thought you'd simply figure it out on your own, but since you haven't, I'll just tell you. Frankly, I resent you putting that chain on because it chokes me when I want to go my own way, and I don't like that one bit! It's not very comfortable, it's demeaning, I feel like you're restricting my freedom of expression and my right which is protected in the Constitution (as I've heard you say) to express my own views."

"Dirty Dog, I wish you had expressed yourself on this issue before. I thought the reason I did that was clear. To be candid, you're still an adolescent and like most kids, on occasion you do get a little rambunctious and take action before you give it much thought. You see, Dirty Dog, it's my responsibility to do for you what is in your long-range best interests. It is not part of my responsibility to let you do what you want when you want, behaving in a way that is not good for you. For example, on this very day we encountered a woman walking a dog about seven times bigger than you. Now, Dirty Dog, as you remember, you strained at the leash to get at that dog. Deep down you knew perfectly well that you would have represented about four good bites for him—and then all of you, including your fur coat, would have been history. By not letting you run over to that dog I simply was making a decision that in the long run was in your best interest. And I can't understand why you don't realize that."

"Well, Dad, you've got to recognize that I have a lot of pride. I knew that you would restrain me because we both understand that I would have been history had I gotten loose. Had I not noticed that you had the leash firmly wrapped around your arm, I never would have made the effort. But I was confident, Dad, that you were going to protect me from harm. I just think you could do it without choking me."

"Dirty Dog, I haven't figured out another way to do it. I've tried the other way and it simply did not work, but I'm glad to know you really didn't want to fight that big dog. I've also noticed that when a car comes by you will often spring forward as if you were going to do battle with the car. I don't know if you knew it or not, but the way English Bulldogs got their flat noses was by chasing parked cars. I don't want that to happen to you, Dirty Dog, I like you the way you are."

"Well, Dad, let me remind you that in every case when I took out after those cars they were already gone. And you and I both know I could never catch them. So your fears are absolutely groundless."

"Then, explain to me why it is that when bicyclists or motorcyclists come by us you do exactly the same thing."

"Well, Dad, you'll have to admit they are closer to my size, and I've even seen a couple of them I think I could handle. So what's the big deal?"

"The big deal, Dirty Dog, is simply this: You're supposed to be a peace-loving dog, a companion. We didn't bring you aboard to be our defender, to attack other animals and people. We brought you in because we felt you would be fun to have around, good to talk to, and overall be a good companion. Now, I will have to admit I had no idea you were also going to turn author on me and coauthor this book, so I'll have to confess your role in the family has expanded. But I don't think it will ever expand to the area where I'll want you attacking motorcyclists, big dogs, and automobiles. So that's the last time this issue is going to be raised. I know you understand, Dirty Dog. (He did understand, but he was too stubborn to admit it.) Besides, that is neither here nor there. We have a leash law in Plano, Texas, and I'm a law-abiding citizen. In my house that makes you a law-abiding dog. Enough said."

Spanked

When I returned home from an overnight trip, I noticed that Dirty Dog was outside, running up and down outside our patio windows, and the Redhead wouldn't let him in. I asked why, and she explained that she was mopping the kitchen floor and he was getting in the way, barking at the mop, and he'd been barking at the vacuum cleaner when she was using it earlier, so she got tired of it and put him outside until she finished. Well, that was understandable because he can be a distraction under those circumstances.

I really thought no more about the matter and went to my office upstairs where I worked for about an hour and a half. Then the Redhead and I went to lunch. After lunch I drove to the corporate office to get an update from

Laurie Magers, my executive assistant for over twenty-seven years, and to pick up my mail. Then I went by the golf course to hit a few balls on the driving range. When I got home I could see that Dirty Dog was looking forlorn and lying in his spot at the window as he frequently does when the Redhead and I leave him at home. He was quiet and obviously in deep thought, so I asked him what he was thinking about.

At first he reluctantly said, "Dad, I really don't want to talk about it."

I said, "Well, Dirty Dog, something's bothering you and, as you know, I have considerable interest in you, so why don't you tell me what the problem is?"

Then he said, "Well, Dad, I've got to talk to you about Mom."

I said, "Well, Dirty Dog, what about Mom? Before you start talking, you do know that your mom and I are very close and whatever you tell me I'm going to share with her. So you just need to be certain that you stick with the facts."

"Well, Dad, I'll try to stick to the facts to the best of my ability, but to tell you the truth, I'm really unhappy and upset at what Mom did, the way she treated me. I don't think it was fair."

And I said, "Well, Dirty Dog, your mom's already told me part of the story, but what are you making reference to?"

He said, "The way she banned me from the house. But, Dad, that's not the worst part of it. Not only did she put me out of the house but she spanked me as well."

And I said, "Well, Dirty Dog, basically, I believe that when kids misbehave, mild corporal punishment is a good approach to take."

"But, Dad, it's never happened before, and I'm certain I've been rebellious along the way and may have deserved it, but starting this late in my life, I felt it was, you know, demeaning to me. You've been complimenting me on my contribution to the book and praising me for the fact that I am a fastidious dog and don't mess things up like some of my dog buddies do, and now, all of a sudden, Mom turns on me. I guess the thing that hurt me so much, Dad, was the fact that I'd spent a lot of time in her lap. I'd made it clear that she was my favorite member of the house and I was her dog. I've even rejected you, Dad, on a couple of occasions, in favor of her. And then this!"

"Well, Dirty Dog, let me say to you that your mom loves you deeply, and anything she does is in your best interest. You know, Dirty Dog, the Bible does say, 'Spare the rod and spoil the child.'"

Dirty Dog said, "Dad, I know that, and actually it wasn't a rod, it was her hand . . . she just spanked me with her hand. Now, you're always patting me with your hand and although your pats are sometimes a little too enthusiastic, I still understand they are not given in anger but in love."

I said, "Well, Dirty Dog, your mother's 'licks' were in love, too. She wants you to be the kind of boy that she'll always be proud of. It is a distraction when you do all of that barking and attacking brooms and mops and vacuum cleaners when she's trying to clean the house. If the doorbell rings, sometimes you're so noisy we can't even hear it!"

"Well, Dad, had Mom explained that to me, I would have stopped. It's kind of like me chasing those big dogs. I know how far to go! All she had to do was say, 'Taffy, (she still calls me by my birth certificate name), if you don't stop, I'm going to spank you and put you outside!'"

And I said, "Well, Dirty Dog, I'll have a talk with her. But to be honest with you, based on what she told me and what you've shared with me, I believe a little corporal punishment was appropriate and though I wish it hadn't been necessary, I believe Mom acted in your best interest."

"OK, Dad, I should have known that you'd take her side."

I said, "Well, Dirty Dog, if I'm not loyal to my mate of fifty-eight years, I'll bet you wouldn't have much confidence I'd be loyal to you if some strange pet—another dog, or a cat even—were to come into this household. I'm certain you would question your own position in the family."

"Yeah, I guess I would, Dad. I know I'll get over it, but it'll just take me a little time."

When I returned to the den after a brief absence, what should I see but Dirty Dog in his mother's lap! Apparently, he was back in good graces, had forgiven his mother, and all seemed to be well. Naturally, I was puzzled about the sudden turn of events, so after a few moments Dirty Dog, sensing my concern, hopped out of his mother's lap, came over and got in mine. So I queried him on the issue. I said, "Dirty Dog, you were pretty upset just a couple of hours ago. What happened?" I'm telling you, I was so proud of his explanation!

He said, "Dad, I realized, after listening to you talk about people who carry grudges and anger for long periods of time before they finally relent, admit their mistake and ask forgiveness, that life is too long to harbor any ill will. And Dad, to be candid, I remember hearing you in a telephone conversation advising someone in a similar situation that he should forgive the person he was in conflict with. You told him that one of these days he would either say 'I wish I had' or 'I'm glad I did.' That really got me to thinking, but the deciding factor was when you said that if we didn't forgive others for what they did to us, God wouldn't forgive us for our sins.

"I realized that I do have a pretty good deal here. Mom always gives me treats, takes care of my physical needs, takes me to the vet (which I hate, but I know I need his services from time to time), and makes certain I'm fed morning and night (something you never seem to do, Dad). She even sees to it that I have fresh water every day, makes certain I have access to the great outdoors so I can exercise some of my freedoms, and all in all, it was not in anybody's best interests for me to carry a grudge. So I forgave her, she kissed me, we made up, and now, as you can see, Dad, everything is better than good. Wouldn't it be neat if more people forgave that quickly and easily, and made up so they could get on with their lives?"

Well, I had to admit that Dirty Dog had made a good decision and I was proud of him. Forgiveness is a wonderful thing. It heals a lot of wounds; opens the door for communication; and makes things a lot better.

Kind and Thoughtful Direction

One morning, as I was drinking my coffee before the Redhead got up, Dirty Dog walked in, sat in front of me, and said, "Last night, Dad, you did it again."

I said, "Did what again?"

He said, "You know, Dad, when I am sound asleep, I mean really sawing those logs, and you come running in clapping your hands and saying, 'Get up, Dirty Dog! It's time to go, gotta go, gotta go!' Well, Dad, of course I hop up because I know what you are up to. You know, you've awakened me by then! So down we go, down the stairs and out in the backyard where I do my thing and then we come back in and back up the stairs we go!"

So I said, "Well, Dirty Dog, what's the problem?"

He said, "I was just wondering, Dad, why do you have to make so much noise to get me up? Couldn't you awaken me gently? I've heard you tell people that if they wake their kids up in the morning gently and lovingly, and show them some affection and consideration, that they will have a better day. And yet here you are, waking me out of a deep sleep not with hugs and caresses and words of encouragement, but 'Let's go, let's go!' Now, Dad, why can't you awaken me like you tell other folks to awaken their kids?"

Well, it was a good question and I had to admit that, but I had a ready explanation. So I said, "Well, Dirty Dog, the truth is you're not exactly a child anymore. As dogs go, you're getting on up past the teen years and, historically speaking, there are many people who, when they hear the clock sound off in the morning, just roll over, turn it off, and go right back to sleep. They're what we call procrastinators. They're going to do it, but they're going to do it later on. But many times, Dirty Dog, it turns out to be never—or they're always late. They're late for school or work or whatever. I learned a long time ago that at the first call if you will immediately get up and go about your business you will get so much more done. And if you remember, even last night, though you were awakened from a sound sleep and though you were wide awake when we came back up the stairs, I could not help but notice that three minutes later there you were, sound asleep, just like you had been before. Now that's a tribute to you, Dirty Dog, that you can so completely shift gears from absolutely sound asleep to wide open, full speed ahead. I commend you for that! And actually, Dirty Dog, if more people, when they hear the alarm or the call, will immediately get up and get busy doing what they've got to do, they'll be lots better off. And so will everybody else. Just want you to know, Dirty Dog, there is a reason and a method to my madness."

I was pleased when he said, quite seriously I might add, "Thank you, Dad. I really appreciate your explaining that to me. It makes sense, so now I do believe that you were acting in my best interest."

I didn't go into any detail about how difficult it some-times is for parents to do what is in the best interests of their children, or in this case, dog, but Dirty Dog knows in his heart that love is what makes doing the right thing possible.

Chapter 6

Protection and Discrimination

Protection

One of the highlights of Dirty Dog's life is when he goes to see his buddy Emmitt or Emmitt comes to see him. Emmitt is my daughter Cindy's big, beautiful Golden Retriever and her constant companion when she's walking. He is extremely protective and, much to her embarrassment, on occasion, she has to restrain him if any other dog or a strange person gets too close to her. It's a comfort to me to know that she always has him with her on her walks and at night when she has to go somewhere in the car. It's only when he feels that Cindy is threatened that he turns aggressive.

When he's with Dirty Dog, Emmitt is the picture of patience and understanding—and those two dogs play together like nothing you've ever seen in your life! Dirty Dog is the attacker. He mauls and abuses Emmitt in an unconscionable way, biting on his ears and legs, just generally making a nuisance of himself but obviously inflicting no pain because Emmitt just rolls over and allows the attack. When he grows weary of Dirty Dog's mauling, Emmitt simply puts his big, old paw on Dirty Dog's back, weights him down—and playtime is over. It's an amusing sight for all of us to behold.

I have to put in a plug here for Dirty Dog. One of his better traits is the fact that he is so family-oriented that he has become an "Alpha dog," a protector. We frequently laugh about the fact that this little guy was able to chase off from his friend Emmitt's house a German Shepherd who appeared fully capable of biting him in two! That was his territory and his friend's house, and he felt a responsibility to defend it.

He has the same attitude at our house. Whenever someone invades his territory he takes it personally and serves notice that he is on guard. We appreciate his attention to every detail of ensuring our safety.

Discrimination

One Sunday, without calling ahead, the Redhead and I drove over to Shreveport, Louisiana, to see her sister, Eurie, who has multiple sclerosis and lives in a nursing home. Eurie was surprised and elated to see us. On this occasion Dirty Dog was with us, and he made an instant hit with everyone. All of the residents crowded around, asking questions about him and reaching out to stroke his soft coat. Much to my surprise, Dirty Dog was a little aloof. He was reluctant to mingle with the strangers. As a result he and I took a little walk and had an extended conversation.

I was very candid with Dirty Dog and told him I was a little disappointed that he wasn't friendlier with all of the people, since they were so friendly to him. Then Dirty Dog explained some things to me that I had not really thought about.

He said, "You know, Dad, I don't know why I acted that way but those people were different from any I've ever met before."

So I asked him if he saw his mother treating them as if they were any different. He confessed that no, he didn't see her treat any of them differently from the way she treats everybody else. He said he noticed that Mom talked with everybody she encountered, called many of them by name, and hugged everyone who was within arm's reach. He even noted that she seemed to have time for everybody. But Dirty Dog said, "You know, Dad, I just felt a little uncomfortable because they seemed so different."

Then it occurred to me that Dirty Dog had had very little, if any, experience with people who suffered any mental disorders. Although Eurie, my sister-in-law, is certainly mentally alert and has only physical problems, many of the people in that home have Alzheimer's, hardening of the arteries, senility, and other forms of mental dementia. Dirty Dog just admitted that he didn't really know what to do or how to act. Then I was a little embarrassed that I had not prepared him for the visit. I should have explained the circumstances and that virtually all of these people had at one time been just like him—young, healthy, mentally alert, excited about life, and looking forward to a glorious future.

So I took a few moments to explain that for reasons most people never come to understand, life dealt those people a different deck of cards, and now they were totally dependent upon others for food, shelter and clothing, love, and emotional support. I also explained to Dirty Dog that, unfortunately, many families have a tendency to neg- lect or even abandon the wife, sister, brother, husband, mother, father, cousin, aunt, or uncle they loved for so many years. Sometimes, I said, there are no other relatives, and sometimes those remaining relatives live so far away or are themselves physically unable to visit or provide the necessary love and support so greatly needed. This, I explained, is when friends, volunteers, church members, and certain social service providers step in to meet the res- idents' needs.

I then reminded Dirty Dog that one of the things his buddy Emmitt does is serve as a therapy dog, and that Cindy takes Emmitt into hospitals where he visits and encourages the patients and residents. This opened a new can of worms, and Dirty Dog wanted to know why he wasn't a therapy dog. I had to explain to him that it takes a special kind of gentleness and lots of training for a dog to qualify, and that his buddy Emmitt had been unable to qualify until very recently, but that he is now thoroughly enjoying it and doing a great job. Then Dirty Dog wanted to know if he could be trained, and if there was a possibility that in the future he could do some of that. Well, this proposal is still on the table because of the time constraints his mother and I have. Right now it would be difficult at best to do the necessary training and visiting on anything approaching a regular basis. Well, this discouraged Dirty Dog, but he promised to be a therapy dog to our youngest granddaughter, Alexandra, even though on occasion she was a little rough with him. He said he really did like playing with her and that he understood she was still very young and didn't realize how rough she was. He hoped that over time they could become real buddies.

I told him that Alexandra couldn't be accused of abuse because of her age but that if I abused him and neglected to give him food and shelter, the general public would really get after me and think I was a horrible person (which I would be if I did those things!). Then I explained that too often people who observe other people abusing someone throw up their arms and say, "Well, what can

I do?" Thankfully, it does seem that more and more people are getting actively involved in helping people who have been abused. They are encouraging our law enforcement people to see to it that the perpetrators of such crimes do not go unpunished.

Then we got back to the subject of folks living in nursing homes. I explained that it is so sad when a person has lived a very productive and useful life, provided for his or her children and even grandchildren, and then, when old age creeps up along with mental, emotional, and physical problems, they are often abandoned by those whom they have served so well for so many years. Dirty Dog wanted to know why on earth anybody would do that, and I said I believed it was because in our society today we're not teaching compassion, love, responsibility, and character to all of our children. We have become too much of a "me-first generation," looking out after self, doing only those things we want to do, and letting others fend for themselves.

Then Dirty Dog made a rather wise observation when he asked, "Dad, won't that lead ultimately to a loss for everyone? Don't people today realize that one day they will be old and possibly physically and/or mentally challenged, and that they, too, might need the kind of help they're now denying members of their own families?"

And again, that's a difficult question, but I responded to Dirty Dog by saying that these people think they'll be young and strong forever, and what's happening all around them will never happen to them. They think they'll never get sick, never have an accident, never become financially destitute and encounter the problems these people have.

Then Dirty Dog asked a very logical question. He said, "Well, Dad, doesn't that mean they're in denial, that they're not reading the papers or watching television, they're not looking around and seeing that it is happening to more and more people? And what makes them think that they've been chosen not to have any of those difficulties?" That, too, was a good question.

I explained that denial is a defense mechanism and a lot of people will say, "I'll face that some day," or "I'll cross that bridge when I get to it."

Dirty Dog responded, "Dad, suppose there's no bridge there, unless they themselves help build that bridge throughout the course of their lifetime?"

Well, again, a challenging question. I explained to Dirty Dog that wise people prepare those bridges before they get to the river that some day they will have to cross.

Then Dirty Dog said, "Well, Dad, I believe I've heard you use the phrase 'as ye sow, so also shall ye reap.' Doesn't that mean that if we are careful to sow good deeds today and plan properly that if we then ever have needs our chances of being cared for would go up?"

I said, "Dirty Dog, you hit the nail on the head. That is the way life is. That's the reason your mother and I, and the rest of the family, are careful to plan, in more ways than one, for the future."

Dirty Dog said, "This is too much, Dad, for one session. I'll need some time to think about and digest all of this information."

I thought he made a good point, so we went back inside the nursing home where he made several friendly overtures to his Aunt Eurie's friends. I was pleased with the change in his behavior.

Chapter 7

Taking Responsibility

*E*mma

I knew something was amiss. Dirty Dog is either sound asleep or he is going full-speed ahead, and his state of deep reflective thought caught me off guard. There was a look of genuine concern on his face, so I opened the conversation by asking if something was troubling him. He was a little hesitant at first, but then he started to open up and before I knew it, the story was spilling forth. He was really upset about an incident that had taken place at my daughter Julie's home.

He said, "Dad, I walked into Julie's home thinking everything was fine and her German Shepherd, Emma, without any provocation, just really took after me. She's lots bigger than I am, and I'm afraid I didn't do a very good job of defending myself. I've heard you talking about steroids and how people who take them bulk up and get stronger and sometimes develop an aggressive streak. I just want to know if that's legal and if it would work for dogs as well as it does for people. While I'm at it, Dad, you know I'm awfully short, and I've discovered there are some serious disadvantages to having short legs! Now, I understand my ancestors were bred this way so they could herd cattle by nipping at their heels, but I'm not out there herding cattle. I'm in the house entertaining you and Mom and protecting you from all dangers by sounding a warning bark when anything or anybody, however harmless they might be, approaches the house or even walks by on the sidewalk. I figure that's one way I earn my keep.

"But these short legs, Dad, other than getting me around pretty fast on sprints when we play chase the toys up and down the hallway, really put me at a disadvantage when I have to defend myself against Emma or other bigger dogs. So I was just wondering if there is any possibility that we could add splints to my legs and make me oh, maybe a foot taller?"

Well, these were serious concerns that Dirty Dog had. While in a way it was a little humorous, it was also very sad. He had been unable to defend himself against a bigger dog, and that bothered him. So I explained to Dirty Dog a couple of things. I said, "First of all, Dirty Dog, steroids are bad news. While athletes who use steroids get bigger, stronger, and more aggressive, they also develop many health problems and die younger after going through excruciating pain in many cases. So that one's out,

Dirty Dog, because we want to keep you around as long as possible. And I would not let you take anything that I knew could be harmful over the long haul."

Then I figured I'd get a little philosophical with Dirty Dog and explain to him that, unfortunately, a lot of people make decisions that appear to benefit them in the short run but destroy them in the long run. That's not good, common sense. I explained to Dirty Dog that when you make a decision, you need to keep in mind not only the immediate benefits, but also consider the long-range consequences, because every choice does have an end result. Steroids are just out.

"As far as getting leg extensions, Dirty Dog, that simply will not work. You've got those short legs for a very good reason. They enable you to get around exceptionally fast to get out of harm's way in most cases. And besides, everybody who sees you comes up and asks what kind of dog you are and what about those short legs? So really, Dirty Dog, I've noticed you enjoy attention and you certainly get lots of it because of those short legs. Not only that, but it would be a medical impossibility to extend your legs in such a way that you could even get around. So I'm sorry, Dirty Dog, you are always going to be short, but you'll always be loved—and, with proper care, which we're doing our best to give you, you will enjoy good health for a long time."

Dirty Dog seemed to accept what I said, even acknowledged that he understood, but at the same time he was obviously troubled, so I pursued the conversation a little further and asked if anything else was bothering him. He acknowledged that it was, that it wouldn't have been so bad if his best friend Emmitt had gotten after him because, after all, Emmitt was a boy and was even bigger than Emma. When he said that I had to chastise him because what he said indicated something that is very troubling. So I said, "Dirty Dog, that sounds like sexist talk to me, when you say it's not as bad when a big boy dog gets after you as it is when a big girl dog gets after you. We've got to understand that sexism has no place in our society, whether it's in the dog world or especially in the people world. The government has even passed laws, Dirty Dog, forbidding sexist behavior, so I don't want to hear another word out of you that even mildly hints at being sexist."

Well, Dirty Dog was properly chastised and apologized for expressing such a thought. But because he was still troubled, I knew I had to come up with a different bit of information, so I said, "Dirty Dog, I've heard it from your side, now I want to hear what Emma has to say about it, because, as you've heard me quote my mother, 'There are always three sides to every story: Your side, the other's side, and the right side.'"

With this in mind, I called Julie, reported my conversation with Dirty Dog to her, and waited for her response. She quickly answered, "Dad, you should tell Dirty Dog that he needs to be careful about his own conduct." I asked her what she meant, and she said, "Well, when Dirty Dog bares his teeth and growls, that's a no-no because Emma fears she's about to be attacked and so she simply takes the initiative and attacks first—which, as I understand it, is dog nature. So please tell Dirty Dog that I know he doesn't have a tail to wag but the next time he comes over if he will smile and turn on his charm (which he's loaded with!), I'm certain Emma will respond in kind."

Sure enough, when I confronted Dirty Dog with the report, he sheepishly admitted that maybe he wasn't overly friendly in his approach to Emma, and he might be a little—not much, but a little—at fault for the reception she gave him. So by use of a little analogy I explained to Dirty Dog what had happened. I said, "You know, Dirty Dog, I always greet people the same way, whether it's nine o'clock in the morning or nine o'clock at night, I always say, 'Good morning.' And 85 percent of people will respond, 'Good morning,' even at nine o'clock at night and then will quickly say, 'But it's not morning!' I respond to that, 'Then why did you say morning?' and they say, 'Because you said morning.' I'll say, 'Yes, and that makes a major point, doesn't it? When you go out in life looking for friends they'll be scarce. When you go out in life to be a friend, you'll find them everywhere because what you send out is what you get back.'" Then I kind of wrapped up that part of the conversation by explaining to Dirty Dog that if he sends out signals that he's about to attack, he can expect to be attacked himself.

Well, even Dirty Dog acknowledged that made sense, and he promised in the future to use an entirely different approach. He said, "Dad, I'll be friendly so that I will get friendly treatment in return."

I carried the conversation a little further.

"There's also something else you need to understand about Emma, Dirty Dog. She was abandoned at the animal shelter when she was two years old, and she still shows some of the signs of that trauma. Did you ever wonder why she's so slender, even skinny, despite the fact that Julie has been almost stuffing her for the last six months? She really did have it pretty tough, Dirty Dog, and as a result, her trust of dogs and people is pretty small. I don't know if she was abused before she was abandoned, but all of those things are a factor. You've heard me talk about the fact that people who abuse their children were often abused as children themselves, and so they're following the example that had been set for them. It's also true that when a young person, even a little child, is mean and abusive to animals, it's a danger signal that needs to be carefully monitored, because research indicates that kids who abuse animals are far more likely to be abusive to children when they are older.

"Now, Dirty Dog, this is not to say that we should go through life always blaming other things and incidents for everything we do wrong. Ultimately, the time comes when each of us, including Emma, must accept responsibility for our behavior. However, sometimes it takes a lot of reaching out to dogs like Emma and people who were abused as children. We need to let them know there are good people who can be trusted, who really do have their best interests at heart.

"You see, Dirty Dog, you were loved from birth. The lady who sold you to us loved you very much and treated you extremely well. And it's embarrassing to say, but we've indulged and spoiled you something fierce. Fortunately, in most cases you've not taken advantage of that. You do have your moments when you act like you own the place—and us—but overall, you've handled the love and affection extremely well. Sometimes when you suddenly jump in your mother's lap she's somewhat startled, but she's always delighted, so the way you've been treated and the way Emma's been treated are quite different. But if we all get together and show Emma that we can be trusted, and if you show her, Dirty Dog, by not baring your teeth at her, by simply being friendly and cordial, and making an effort to get acquainted with her, who knows, she might turn out to be one of the best friends and buddies you've ever had! I've seen it happen many times, but it does take somebody to make the first move. You make the first move—who knows, you might even have to make the second, the third, and even the fourth move—but in the long run, Dirty Dog, it'll be worth it."

Apologize and Accept Responsibility

It was nearly ten o'clock one evening when I returned home after a lengthy meeting at church. Instead of an excited, highly-motivated dog greeting me, Dirty Dog was in a foul mood if I've ever seen one. He was angry, sulky, acting like he didn't know me, and so naturally I asked him what the problem was.

He said, "Well, Dad, you certainly ought to know. Mom's out of town and you know this diet you've got me on would starve a puppy and you left home shortly after five o'clock and here it is nearly ten o'clock and I've not had a bite to eat since that pitifully small breakfast Mom served me this morning at seven o'clock."

Then I understood where he was coming from, proceeded to apologize profusely, and gave him the food I should have given him before I left at shortly after five. Dirty Dog didn't say a thing. He just gobbled it up and walked away without comment. I said, "Wait a minute,

Dirty Dog. I have apologized profusely; I have given you your dinner; I have asked you to forgive me. Now what's the problem?"

Dirty Dog was reluctant to talk but he finally said, "Dad, that's one of your problems. You starve me for several hours and then you think all you've got to do is give me something to eat and apologize, and I'm going to be excited and happy, come hop in your lap, and invite you to play with me. Dad, that's just not the way dogs think."

Then I asked him, "Well, Dirty Dog, what more can I do?"

He said, "Well, you can start over, apologize again, and feed me again."

And I said, "Dirty Dog, as you know, if you gain weight over the long haul, it's not going to be good for you."

He said, "There you go again, Dad, giving me a lecture when I'm still hungry."

I said, "Well, Dirty Dog, if you remember, I also gave you a couple of the treats that you cherish so much. You didn't even say thank you for that!"

And Dirty Dog responded, "Well, yeah, that is true. But Dad, this is serious business and, to be honest, I don't know if I'm going to be able to forgive you so quickly or not."

Then I said, "Dirty Dog, you're acting like a bunch of people I know."

He said, "What do you mean?"

And I said, "Well, you know, Dirty Dog, there are some people who carry grudges, anger, and bitterness for years and years, refusing to forgive the wrongdoer, and that's serious because until you forgive the wrongdoer, that person (or dog) is in control of you." Dirty Dog asked, "What do you mean?"

I said, "Well, you spend a good deal of your time thinking about that 'bad guy,' about getting revenge or maintaining your anger. In short, that other person or dog is controlling your thinking. I can tell you right now, Dirty Dog, as you know, we're hopeful you're going to be living around here a long time. The longer you wait to forgive me, the more miserable you're going to be in the meantime. Besides that, look at the time that's being wasted. Instead of our being able to enjoy our time together, your anger is keeping a distance between us. Whereas if you forgive me now, we make friends and start playing again, you'll be happier, I'll be happier, and our time together will be enjoyable for both of us."

He said, "Well, Dad, let me think about that for a few minutes. What you're saying makes sense. I certainly hope I'm around for quite a while because you and Mom are good to me—especially Mom." And with that he walked off and said he'd sleep on it.

When I awoke the next morning I was greeted by a highly motivated, very enthusiastic Dirty Dog. He was grinning from ear to ear, indicating that all had been forgiven. I said, "Well, Dirty Dog, what made you change your mind and your attitude so dramatically?"

He said, "You were right, Dad. I decided to go ahead and forgive you, and immediately I felt better. So that's the whole story in a simple nutshell. One thing you said, Dad, really got to me."

I said, "What was that?"

He said, "You told me that one of these days I would either say to myself 'I wish I had,' or 'I'm glad I did,' and the more I thought about that the more sense it made, so I said, 'Shucks, after all, Dad does provide me food and shelter and a good environment to live in, takes me for walks and rides, lets me play with my buddy Emmitt, and do a number of other things I know some dogs just don't get to do.'

"Something else you said, Dad, kinda got to me, and although you explained you knew more about psychology than dogology, you said that with people, when they do forgive somebody it can be kind of dangerous. That puzzled me, so I asked you what you meant and you said, 'Well, when you forgive somebody for a wrong they've done to you, regardless of how minor or major it might have been, then you give up any thoughts or feelings of revenge.' And that's OK. But the thing that you said that I wrestled with a lot was that forgiving means you've also given up any excuses, that it is not OK to blame others for problems of the past, and that when you forgive that means you accept responsibility for your future, and that you can no longer blame anyone else for the problems that arise in your life. If you have problems it's not because of what somebody else did to you in the dimly distant past; it's difficulties you yourself have created by your own choices and conduct. And I simply decided, Dad, that I am willing to accept responsibility for my conduct, my attitude, and my future, and it really made me feel good when I did that."

My only comment was, "Dirty Dog, I'm mighty proud of you, and I know that our future together is going to be better and better."

*L*ittle Dogs Can Have Big Ears

Dirty Dog looked up at me with sad eyes and said, "Dad, I can't believe what you said before you left for your walk!"

By then I had forgotten what I'd said. As I often say, I have a brilliant memory but it's awfully short, so I asked him what it was I had said.

He responded in a pitiful tone, "Dad, I heard you say to Mom, after she asked if you were going to take me on your walk, that I was too much trouble, that you really wanted just to walk and not be bothered. That cut me to the core, Dad. During these past few months as we've been writing our book, you have said so many nice things about me, and then for you to say that I was too much trouble, I just couldn't believe my ears. And don't give me that old saw about 'You had no idea I was listening,' because I've heard you say both here at home and on your recordings as well as in your books that we all must remember that 'the lights are always on and the microphone is always open.' Now, Dad, if I understand that correctly, you're saying that our conversations and attitudes should not flip-flop as we discuss issues, people, and things. I know you would not have looked me in the face and said that. After all the other things you've said about me, that would have been obviously hypocritical. But what you did was even more hypocritical. You didn't know I was listening, so you felt free to say it."

Well, dear readers, I'll have to confess I had no place to hide, no excuse. No line of rationale could possibly explain the hurt I had inflicted on Dirty Dog. No, it was cut and dried, black and white. I had committed a grievous error. There was no way I could deny it even if I wanted to, so I took the only way out—which really wasn't an out. At least at that point I did not feel that I was trying to evade or avoid the issue. I said, "Dirty Dog, you're absolutely right. I was 100 percent wrong. It was a huge mistake, and I don't really know why I said it but I was wrong—dead wrong, Dirty Dog, because I enjoy our walks 99 percent of the time. Actually, Dirty Dog, it's 100 percent of the time. So I'm puzzled at myself as to why I said what I did. I'm also embarrassed to admit I've made that kind of mistake with my other four children and my grandchildren. I guess the only thing I can fall back on is that it goes back to man's sinful nature inherited from Adam, and that certainly was classic proof of the statement that none of us is perfect.

"I was wrong and I'm terribly sorry. I'm asking you to forgive me, and I promise I will never say anything like that again, either to you—or about you. It was hypocritical, and a hypocrite by one definition is a person who gripes, and complains about the sex, nudity, and violence on his VCR. In this case, Dirty Dog, I was even worse than that. But it won't happen again. Will you forgive me?"

Dirty Dog, being the loving, forgiving dog that he is, enthusiastically responded that he would forgive me. Then he elaborated and said, "You know, Dad, I've also heard you say before that some parents are reluctant to admit their mistakes before their kids and to ask forgiveness for their offenses. But in your own defense I've also heard you say that's foolish because any child knows his or her parents are only human and are going to make mistakes. Instead of weakening their authority over the child, acknowledging shortcomings increases their authority because it demonstrates real love and compassion. Those are two qualities that are important in any parent-child relationship. So, Dad, you're not only forgiven, but I promise I won't bring it up again."

I was grateful and relieved. The relationship had been preserved and will include lots more walks together. I'm excited about that because it's generally on our walks that Dirty Dog comes out with his words of wisdom.

Over the years it has been my experience that accepting responsibility for my behavior and decisions has done more positive things for my relationships with others than anything else. Teaching this concept to those under your care is crucial to their future happiness—and yours.

Chapter 8

Jealousy

Envy and Dirty Dog

Some things you just know immediately, and when Dirty Dog walked into my office his pace was considerably faster than normal. He lay down at my feet and looked up at me with those soulful eyes of his and in no uncertain terms said, "Dad, we need to talk—bad—right now." He had my undivided attention, so I asked him what was on his mind.

He said, "Dad, it's about Emmitt."

I said, "What about Emmitt?"

He said, "Well, these last three days with him have been unbearable! I cannot believe his incessant talking about what *he's* doing at the hospitals and some of the nursing homes he visits, and about how *he* inspired Cindy to expand her therapy ministry throughout fellowshipchurch.com and now, Dad, he's even saying it was *his* idea to start the Paws To Go ministry. And that's all Emmitt has talked about, how they went to this hospital and did this, how they went to another hospital and did that, this nursing home, that nursing home. Dad, I'm just sick and tired of it!"

I said, "Well, Dirty Dog, that surprises me! I thought first of all that you and Emmitt were big buddies; second, that you would be thrilled that he and Cindy have been doing some really neat things to help people who need therapy or even just new friends."

His response was, "Aw, I know that, Dad, and I can understand why Emmitt would be a little uppity about it, but Dad, enough is enough is *enough*!"

At that point I interrupted him to say, "Dirty Dog, it sounds to me like you're just plain jealous, and jealousy is not a very healthy emotion to carry around. As a matter of fact, it will eat you up. Just to make certain I'm on sound ground, I'm going to tell you what my trusty 1828 Noah Webster's dictionary says about jealousy. It says, 'It is that passion or peculiar uneasiness which arises from the fear that a rival may rob us of the affection of one whom we love, or the suspicion that he has already done it. Or it is the uneasiness which arises from the fear that another does or will enjoy some advantage which we desire for ourselves.' In short, Dirty Dog, jealousy is awakened by whatever may exalt others, give them pleasures and advantages which we desire for ourselves. In a nutshell, Dirty Dog, left unchecked, jealousy grows quickly and leads to serious sins. The longer you cultivate jealous feelings, the harder it is to uproot them. The time to deal with jealousy is when you notice yourself keeping score of what others have or do. And Dirty Dog, that's what concerns me. You are headed in the wrong direction!"

"Well, Dad, this has taken a turn I did not expect when I came in. I thought you would be more empathetic to my situation."

"Dirty Dog, discipline is something you do *for* some-one whereas punishment is something you do *to* someone. I want to discipline your thought life, and your jealousy is something I have never seen before. You've always seemed so secure, knowing that we love you, that Cindy loves you, that Emmitt is your best buddy, and you know for a fact that if a big dog jumped on you, Emmitt would immedi-ately come to your defense because you're smaller than he is and smaller than most dogs!"

"I know all of that, Dad!" Dirty Dog responded, "But I guess you're right, I am just jealous of what Emmitt is doing. And then he brags about it, Dad. I think that's the part that gets to me!"

I recognized that the problem was really serious, so I said, "Dirty Dog, I know that you and I have talked about this before. The reason you're not a therapy dog is that therapy dogs need to like everyone and your taste in people is more discerning than Emmitt's is."

At that point Dirty Dog interrupted me and said, "Well, Dad, can't I pick and choose who I visit with?"

I assured Dirty Dog that the odds on that would be very small. Then I said to Dirty Dog, "What you need to be is a cheerleader, so you can cheer Emmitt on and encourage him in what he's doing. I'm going to read you a few of the results of what Emmitt is doing, and this is what Aunt Cindy wrote:

One of Emmitt's favorite places to visit is the psychiatric floor, since we visit patients in a group setting and he gets to do "his thing" by going from person to person. One day there was a young black man sitting on the end of the couch all alone with his head down. Because he was severely depressed and suicidal, he didn't even look up when we entered the room. He ignored Emmitt when he went over to check out the young man. Emmitt made his rounds and ended up back at the couch with the young man. He decided to hop up on the couch right beside him and put his head in the man's lap. Emmitt looked up at the young man as if to say, "Don't you just want to pet me on my soft head?" The man sat perfectly still, ignoring Emmitt. The group started a discussion about dogs and time passed. Emmitt stayed right next to the young man, which is unusual since he always tries to be sociable and visit with everyone. Slowly but surely the young man's hand lifted and he started to gently stroke Emmitt's head. Next he was stroking his body. Then a smile appeared. I gave Emmitt his tennis ball and the young man took it from him and started throwing it so Emmitt could run and get it and bring it back. By the end of our session, the young man was laughing and having a great time with Emmitt. The therapist that had been working with him was thrilled and said that was the first positive reaction she had seen from this profoundly depressed young man.

Tuesday morning is our time to visit a local children's hospital. Emmitt adores being with the children. Because he is very gentle and patient when working with the children, he automatically lies down when he sees a child so he can "get on their level." On this particular visit a therapist was "stretching" the limbs of a young boy who was recovering after being in a coma. Even though the boy was crying he took a mild interest in Emmitt so we decided to work with the therapist to take the boy's mind off the painful stretching. I gave the boy a beanbag and he held it out to Emmitt. Emmitt opened his

mouth very slowly to take it from the boy and
the boy pulled it back out of his reach and
started to giggle. It became a game for him. Over
and over the boy would pull the beanbag away
just as Emmitt would start to take it. The little
boy was so intent on not letting Emmitt get the
beanbag he soon forgot about the therapist and
the stretching. Emmitt was as patient as I've ever
seen him. In a few minutes the boy's treatment
was over, and he was still giggling at Emmitt.

On another occasion we were working in the
rehabilitation area of a hospital and met a family
whose son was coming out of a coma after being
in a motorcycle accident. He seemed to be
"stuck" in a phase, and everyone was trying to
figure out a way to make him "come out of it,"
so his progress could continue. The young man
would stare straight ahead, his eyes seeming to
be permanently fixed. His mother told me that
they had put their Golden Retriever to sleep
right before her son's accident. They were mar-
veling at how much Emmitt looked like their
dog. We decided to find out if seeing Emmitt
could stir something in the young man. He was
tilted back in a wheelchair, and Emmitt got up
about eye level with him. All of a sudden his eyes

looked around to the side where Emmitt was.
This was the beginning of his starting to "track,"
meaning that he was now following movement.
It brought him out of being "stuck" and helped
him to progress. Everyone was thrilled, and
mother and father had tears in their eyes. He and
Emmitt became good friends over the next several months and they keep in touch even to this
day. When the young man got home he got a
Golden Retriever puppy that is his new best
friend.

"Dirty Dog, surely you would not want Emmitt and
Cindy to stop because—look at the tremendous good they
are doing, just with these three people—and there are
dozens and dozens more. It's a wonderful ministry. So
here's what I think you should do, Dirty Dog. First,
I think you should go to Emmitt and apologize. Tell him
you're sorry you've had that advanced case of stinkin'
thinkin' that led to jealousy, but that never having been
invited to go on a trip into one of the hospitals you never
fully understood what he was doing. Tell Emmitt that you
are proud of him, that you love him, and that you only
wish you could participate with him in his ministry to
the ill, injured, and lonely. I believe it will dramatically
improve your relationship with Emmitt and that both of
you will be better dogs because of it.

"Let me say, Dirty Dog, that I understand your feelings. All of us want to make a contribution; we want to participate and be recognized for what we do—and that's completely understandable. It is even human nature (and dog nature, too!), and since you think you're a person I just don't want you to take it to the next step, Dirty Dog. You know, cats think they are God, and that would be unacceptable around here—or anywhere else for that matter!

"One last thing, Dirty Dog. I know this is going to seem somewhat off the topic but as you know, I talk a lot about my 'Wall of Gratitude,' photographs of the twenty-six men and women who have played huge roles in my life. Interestingly enough, with those who were still living when I realized fully what they had meant to me, each one of them expressed their appreciation for the fact that I had thanked them by recognizing them for the role they played and the contribution they had made in my life. As you undoubtedly know, Dirty Dog, the six people who had the biggest impact on my life were all women. Just think what my life would have been like had I been sexist! And minorities were really important to me. Three American Indians, for example, played a huge role—one in my sales career, one in my speaking career, and one in my spiritual walk. And as you undoubtedly know because you've been listening to our conversations for a long time, an elderly black lady who spent the weekend in our home on July 4, 1972, is the reason I'm a Christian.

"My closest friend for over forty years is a member of the Jewish faith from Winnipeg, Canada. He was the first man who believed I had a future as a speaker. Of course, my favorite writers were all Jews—Moses, Abraham, Solomon, Isaiah, Matthew, Mark, John, Paul . . . you get the idea, Dirty Dog. Our director of international operations is from India. I'm the national spokesperson and honorary chairman for Nikken International, a large Japanese company with a Korean president. My daughter-in-law, Chachis, whom I lovingly call Bonita, is from Campeche, Mexico. Just suppose, Dirty Dog, I had been racist. My life would have been radically different from what it is today."

At this point Dirty Dog interrupted me to say, "Well, Dad, I don't quite understand what you're getting at now."

"Let me explain. Your portrait is hanging in our home in a very prominent spot. It's right there in our living room, Dirty Dog, and when we have company everybody sees it and they often ask, 'Who's that? What role does he play in the Ziglar family?'

"Yours is the only portrait I have on my Wall of Gratitude at home. You're in an exclusive spot, and I just want you to know, Dirty Dog, we really do love you. And when you clearly understand your relationship with

Emmitt and how important it is to both of you, and for that matter how important your relationship is with others, then I believe the jealousy will be eliminated and you'll talk with pride about all the wonderful things Emmitt and Cindy do. And who knows, Dirty Dog, maybe because of this contribution you're making there will be people all over the country who will say, 'Boy! Maybe that's something I should get involved in!' You see, when Cindy saw how dogs change the way people feel and act she loved the results so much she started a ministry in her church that now includes over twenty-five dogs. Just think, Dirty Dog, when you tell your doggie buddies about Emmitt, you can really 'put on the dog' telling them about the wonderful things he's doing."

I conclude by saying an entirely different Dirty Dog was the result of all of this . . . and boy, am I ever glad we had that conversation because I believe Dirty Dog has just taught us a lesson on jealousy that will improve every facet of our lives.

Chapter 9

Relationships

*J*ust out of curiosity I asked Dirty Dog why it is that he can appear to be zonked out in the evening while his mother and I visit and sometimes watch TV, but the instant she crawls into bed he hops up and runs over and lies down right by her side of the bed. I wanted to know why he never sleeps on my side of the bed. This is the part that hurts, but I find Dirty Dog to be completely reliable, honest, open and above board, so I'm taking his message to heart and reporting it as he described it.

He said, "Dad, I get the feeling that you give me attention only when you want something from me, like to help you write the book, take a walk, or show me off to some of your friends with our rope game of running up and down the hallway. I get the idea that all of that's for your benefit and not mine. Now, Mom is the one who gives me all the treats. She immediately gives me attention when she returns home, but when you come home you often walk by me with hardly a word. Then when we sit down, she sits on the sofa and invites, even encourages me to join her.

When she lies down to take a nap on the sofa, I hop up and she lets me lie on her and take my nap while she's taking hers. It's a rare occasion when you permit me to hop up in your lap, and then you don't let me stay long. In short, Dad—Mom, over a period of time, has built a relationship with me that I feel is centered around the fact that she's not my part-time mother. She loves me all the time."

To tell you the truth, that really did hurt, but I can easily see where he has a point. I explained to him that I'm the one who goes out to make a living and pay the bills. But he said, "Dad, that's a cop-out. I hear you telling people all the time that relationships are the key to happiness, and that nearly 100 percent of all counseling takes place as a result of problems in relationships. Well, Dad, I want more than a little petting and a rare treat from you; I want to establish a relationship like you and Mom have. I notice you never ignore her, you're always hugging on her, you open the door for her, and you won't let her lift anything too heavy. In short, Dad, it seems to me that you're courting her all the time, but you court me only when it's convenient or beneficial for you. Is it too much to ask for you to pay attention to me, too?"

I had to admit that his request was legitimate and I knew that his health and mine would be better as a result of the improved relationship. Dr. Dean Ornish of Harvard, after a twenty-year study, concluded that relationships are more important to our physical health than the foods we eat, the exercise program we are on, and even the genes we have inherited, so yes, relationships are critical to our health.

To emphasize the importance of relationships, I told Dirty Dog why I considered teaching my Sunday school class the most fun and important thing I do. I explained to him that my relationship with Christ is the most important relationship I have. Then I elaborated by saying that since as the teacher I do virtually all of the talking in the class, the people who attend have very little chance to become acquainted with one another, so to make certain we are not missing out on anything, we started going to lunch together after church. Sometimes as many as seventy-five of the Sunday school attendees go to a pre-selected restaurant; most of the time attendance is in the range of thirty to forty people. We encourage everyone to sit with people they don't already know and at tables that generally seat from four to a dozen people so they can get acquainted with one another and develop new friendships.

Another way our Sunday school class develops deeper relationships is through the Bible studies that are held in individual homes every other week. In a home setting people get to know one another very well as friends and fellow Christians. The question-and-answer portions of the studies enable former strangers to become interested in the personal, family, and business lives of one another. And in times of need those friendships are very important. Yes, Dirty Dog, relationships do count.

Compromise in Marriage

"Dirty Dog, people who build happy, healthy marriages and raise happy, healthy families are willing to compromise on what they want without compromising their integrity."

"What do you mean by that, Dad?"

"Well, as a simple example, we eat out quite often because a number of years ago your mom explained to me that she had proved to everyone's complete satisfaction that she was a marvelous cook, that she could cook anything she wanted to. She had nothing else to prove; therefore, why don't we just eat out? So, Dirty Dog, we eat out a lot and, to tell you the truth, I like to take your mom out and show her off. She is so pretty, and such a gracious lady, that I'm just so proud to be with and around her. And I like for others to see that ol' Dad has really done good! As a matter of fact, you've heard me say many times I just flat overmarried."

"Well, Dad, that's interesting, but what's the point?"

"Sometimes when we get in the car to eat out we have no idea where we're going. Sometimes she wants to go to a particular place, but other times she doesn't know which one and I fit into the same category, so suggestions are made. Sometimes she will suggest a place that, frankly, Dirty Dog, I don't like. Sometimes I suggest a place that she doesn't necessarily like."

Then Dirty Dog asked the obvious question, "So what do you do?"

I responded, "Well, sometimes I say, 'Well, Sweetheart, if that's where you want to go, let's go!' Other times she will say, 'Well, Honey, if that's where you want to go, we'll go. Last time I chose a place, you choose this time.' And we'll go sometimes to a restaurant that one of us really doesn't want to go to, yet our relationship and our love is much more important than a meal that will be eaten and forgotten before the day is over. But the relationship and our love for each other is something we recognized years ago that we need to preserve at all costs.

"You see, Dirty Dog, people who are selfish and self-centered always want their way. They will maneuver, manipulate, pout, sulk, become angry, and do many other childish things if they don't get their way. They are neither giving nor forgiving, and it takes only one partner in the marriage to foul up the relationship completely. Although in most cases both contribute, often the selfish one who demands his or her own way creates problems that breed tension in the marriage. Your mom and I, when we do disagree, are not disagreeable, and any wrong that is committed is quickly forgiven and truly forgotten."

"Well, I'm certainly glad you explained that to me, Dad, because it helps me to understand why you and Mom are so happy together and have so much fun and so many friends. More importantly, Dad, you have certainly been good role models for your kids to follow, and the way you treat each other influences the way they treat their own spouses."

"Well, Dirty Dog, that certainly is an astute observation, but then your mom has always said you are one more smart boy!"

"Thanks Dad. And while I'm thinking about it I wanted to tell you that I've noticed that you're always saying nice things about me and your other children and I've been told you brag on me a lot in public. The thought occurred to me that I have never really said how much I appreciate you and the way you've treated me over the years. I particularly appreciate that you're not like so many of my friends' parents who, for whatever silly reason, insist on talking to their dogs as if they were infants, using 'baby talk.' It gripes me to no end to hear otherwise intelligent adults take that approach to communicating with the pets they vow they love.

"Dad, I appreciate the straightforward and, in most cases, encouraging and educational conversations we've had. I want you to know it pleases me very much that you've treated me with courtesy and respect. Even when

I've felt you were a little hard on me, I ultimately realized that your language was that of love and concern, and that you were acting in my best interests.

"When I was a newcomer to our home and a little uncertain about my status in the family, you made me feel welcome. Not as much as Mom did, but nevertheless I had a sense of peace and security. I could tell this home was filled with love and that you would treat me fairly and with respect. Frankly, Dad, I've not been disappointed."

Highlight the Positive

One evening when I came in from an out-of-town trip Dirty Dog was standing there at the door, awaiting my arrival, welcoming me. He'd have been wagging his tail if he had a tail to wag, but the smiley eyes and the expression on his face clearly told me he was glad to see me home. So I engaged him in conversation immediately and said, "Dirty Dog, what are you so happy about?"

"Well, Dad," he said, "I'm just glad you're home. You know, this little game we recently started playing is lots of fun, and somehow or another Mom just hasn't caught on to it."

I said, "Which game are you talking about, Dirty Dog?"

He said, "Oh, you know, the one where you'll pretend that we're both going outside and I always run ahead and then you close the door and stay inside. Then you start walking toward the door and, of course, I chase you. You take about three steps and you stop but I keep going. Then I realize you're not there and I turn around and come running back, and we repeat that about a dozen times. It really is a marvelous workout, Dad, and I really enjoy it! Actually, I enjoy it as much as chasing the bone you throw up and down the hall inside the house all the time. Just want you to know, Dad, that occasionally you do something right."

Well, that really pleased me because Dirty Dog often complains and talks about things that he's not happy with, so it was neat to hear him take the positive approach, and I thanked him profusely for it. "As a matter of fact," I said, "let's go back to the kitchen, Dirty Dog, I've got a couple of treats for you." You know I scored big points with him. And isn't that the way it's supposed to be? Parent and child are supposed to encourage and support each other. That's what we were doing. But isn't that what husbands and wives also should do, and siblings, and friends, and coworkers? Think about it. Dirty Dog did. He's glad he took the action he did.

Relationships are what make life worth living. Take good care of yours.

Chapter 10

Hurt? Hang in There

What's in a Name

Dirty Dog had been quiet the entire morning so I asked him what was bothering him. He replied, "Well, Dad, just to be honest, I've been thinking about what you call me. 'Dirty Dog' raises questions in my mind. I understand from Mom that on my birth certificate it shows that my official name is 'Laffy Taffy.' What gives, Dad? I need to know, for my own peace of mind and self-satisfaction, why you call me that."

"Well, Dirty Dog, let me explain something to you. Surely you have noticed that I seldom call anybody by their given names. For example, I call your mother 'Sugar Baby.' When Suzan was alive I called her 'Doll.' I call Cindy 'Sweetnin,' and Julie, 'Little One.' I call Tom 'Son,' and while that's not exactly a nickname it is not his given name, either. Oh, I'll admit on occasion I do use a regular name, just like I sometimes call you 'Taffy.' But let me also remind you that I have nicknamed all of my grandchildren. I call

Amanda 'Sunshine.' I call Katherine 'Keeper,' Elizabeth 'Little Lover,' and Alexandra 'Promise.'"

"Well, Dad, what does that have to do with calling me 'Dirty Dog'? Somehow or another I think 'Dirty Dog' sounds kind of negative, like it means something bad."

"No, Dirty Dog, it's an endearment that I place upon you."

"Well, Dad, I've heard you talk about 'dirty old men,' so somehow or another 'Dirty' just doesn't seem like something I want to be called."

So I said, "Well, Dirty Dog, let me explain. In that case, the insinuation is that here is a member of the male sex who has dishonorable intentions as far as pretty young women are concerned. I might also add there are lots more dirty *young* men than dirty old men! And that's not just because there are some people who would say that I am being prejudiced because I happen to be a 'senior citizen' who has celebated the fifty-seventh anniversary of his twenty-first birthday."

"Well, Dad, when you say 'dirty old man' or 'dirty young man' and 'less than honorable intentions' as far as members of the opposite sex are concerned, what are you talking about?"

"I'm actually talking about a sexual relationship, Dirty Dog. You've heard us all talk enough times about what God tells us—that any sexual relationship except that of husband and wife is sin and is not permissible. But it's a particularly heinous crime if a child is involved and we call that sexual perpetrator a 'pedophile.' That is especially hard because in many cases, if not all of them, such behavior completely destroys that child for years and sometimes for life. The crime is so traumatic, the damage so extensive, that sometimes even years of counseling are not enough to restore that child to what we would consider a normal, healthy relationship with a husband or wife. There are exceptions, of course, but the law really takes a dim view of any kind of forced relationship between two people involved in a sexual activity."

"This is getting pretty involved, Dad. I'm not certain I understand everything you're saying. What does all of this have to do with you calling me 'Dirty Dog'?"

"Well, Dirty Dog, I'm simply trying to explain that I'm not accusing you of any misconduct and, actually, 'Dirty Dog' is a term of endearment. I'm sure you've noticed the tone of voice I use when I address you by that name. It's always with affection. You might notice I even call you 'Dirty Dog' when I pick you up from your appointment with the groomer. So I'm certainly not accusing you of being physically dirty, and ever since your trip to the veterinarian, the one where you had to stay overnight, I have no reason to accuse you of any immoral intentions as far as little girl dogs are concerned. No, Dirty

Dog, your nickname is not meant in any way to 'put you down.'

"In all fairness, I feel I need to relieve your mind once and for all about the way your name came about. I'm embarrassed to admit it, since you've been so much fun to have around, but for many years I had been making the statement that there would be no more pets around my house. I had done a little 'halo-adjusting' throughout the years the children were growing up, and I tolerated everything from chipmunks to cats, dogs, squirrels, and skunks. But when the last one died, a cat we all loved very much (we called him "B.W. Person," as in "Black and White Person"), I said 'no more pets—that's it.'

"Well, when your mother saw that floppy ear of yours and the way you cocked your head and smiled at her, you proved to be irresistible. All my talk about us not having any more pets went right out the window, and your mom made the deal to bring you home on the spot. She had been telling me that she really thought she might like a Welsh Corgi, so it wasn't *that* big of a surprise when she told me what she'd done. But I'll have to confess that I wasn't very excited. I felt like I was just humoring your mother so that I could be a 'good guy,' an understanding husband, and score a few points. However, Dirty Dog, when you walked in wagging that tail you don't even have and immediately put on your best behavior, I decided maybe you weren't going to be all bad. As a matter of fact, you wormed your way right into my heart. And I'll have to tell you when I called you "Dirty Dog," your mom and Cindy and Julie really laughed because they knew you had won the battle. It was obvious that I had fallen for you hook, line, and sinker because I give nicknames only to people I genuinely love. I believe we've had a good relationship ever since, and I confess that you're lots of fun to be around.

"I also believe, Dirty Dog, that the Lord put you in our lives when He did because He knew that Suzan would soon be leaving us to join Him. I believe it was part of His plan that you would serve as a distraction as well as a source of enjoyment and comfort for your mother and me. Cindy, Julie, and Tom have all told your mom and me how glad they were we had you to laugh at and to hug and hold when we were grieving so much over Suzan. I'm glad it worked out that way, Dirty Dog."

Dirty Dog's Surgery

We're not sure how it happened, but one day our little Dirty Dog injured his right leg. We took him to see the veterinarian and were told his hip was in a position where it was rubbing directly against the femur bone. The doctor assured us that an operation would restore him to almost 100 percent function, but that he would grow progressively worse without the surgery. Of course we opted for the surgery.

The following morning we went to pick up Dirty Dog and bring him home. When the attendant brought him out to us he demanded, "Dad, what on earth happened? When Mom left me here yesterday I felt abandoned. That man who picked me up and moved me to a table was kind and pleasant and seemed like a genuinely nice fellow. When he stuck me with that little needle it didn't hurt at all, but when I woke up I couldn't remember where I was. I guess I was in a daze because at the time I didn't even notice there was a huge bandage on my leg and much of the hair on my right rear had been shaved off, exposing me to the world!"

"Well, Dirty Dog, I have to tell you that you had a little surgical procedure, and it was done so you will be able to run and play. Do you remember that we haven't been running you up and down the hall, chasing your bone, for the last two weeks?"

Dirty Dog responded that yes, he had noticed that and, frankly, he thought I was upset with him. "I thought you were ignoring me, and I knew I hadn't done anything wrong. I was up to my usual good behavior, just having fun as most of your kids do. But, Dad, was this operation really necessary?"

"Yes, it was, Dirty Dog, it was either that or you would grow progressively worse and we would never be able to run up and down and play chase and have all the fun we've had. We wouldn't be able to take those long walks where you protect me from the vicious dogs we periodically encounter. We couldn't have those nice talks that we generally have while we're on our walks, and both of us would have been worse off."

"OK, Dad, that sounds reasonable. But, man alive! This thing hurts!"

"Well, Dirty Dog, I know it must hurt, but the medicine we're giving you should take care of most of the pain."

"Well, the pain itself, Dad, is just part of it. I'm embarrassed. I just hope none of my friends see me. I'm glad Emmitt hasn't been by because he would have laughed uproariously at the condition I'm now in. It's embarrassing, Dad! Don't you have some kind of coat or jacket or something that we can cover me with so that I won't be exposed for everyone who comes by to see?"

"No, Dirty Dog, the doctor says that you don't need to be encumbered with any additional garments, so that the hair will have a chance to grow back normally and your leg will heal as it should."

In a small way, that seemed to satisfy Dirty Dog, but I'm confident we'll have more conversations later about this issue—especially the fact that we're taking lots of pictures as if we want to parade his embarrassment to the world at a later date! He indicated that was not fair. As a matter of fact, it was in his opinion "cruel and inhumane"—or at least, "indogmane."

*L*ake Plans

It was one of those beautiful fall evenings. The Redhead had gone to the store to pick up a few items, and Dirty Dog and I were down by the lake behind our home. We walked around for a few minutes, and then he suggested that we go back to the patio area and just talk. Well, I knew he had something on his mind that was pretty serious, at least for him, so that's what we did.

As I sat down, Dirty Dog lay on the diving board by the swimming pool and said, "Dad, I need to ask you a question. I'm a little puzzled. I frequently hear you and Mom talk about going to Sugarville, your home at the lake in East Texas, and yet you almost never go. Why is that?"

"To be honest, I don't really know, Dirty Dog. It seems I let my mouth frequently overload my back by making too many commitments, and the time just never exists."

"Well, Dad, correct me if I'm wrong, but I believe I've heard you say on numerous occasions that you really love that place and when you get away from the hustle and bustle of your regular routine you are able to get more done, particularly of a creative nature, than you normally get done at our home in Dallas. Why don't you go more often?"

"Well, Dirty Dog, you've already asked that question. I guess I really don't have a logical answer, which is a little embarrassing because I like to think I am logical. It seems that the tyranny of the urgent takes over and gets in the way of what's really important, and I don't schedule my time at the lake."

"Well, Dad, I don't want to embarrass you, but I've heard you say that you set your own schedule, so why don't you simply schedule more time where you are most efficient and get the most work done?"

"Ouch! Dirty Dog, you really are getting personal and intrusive!"

"Just trying to help, Dad, that's all."

"Well, Dirty Dog, to be honest, my executive assistant Laurie Magers has looked me in the eye and had me practicing the magic phrase, 'Call Miss Laurie.' She tells me that when people come up with all the requests they make of me that don't fit into our mission statement and I'm too chicken to say no, all I have to do is say, 'Call Miss Laurie.' She assures me that she doesn't have the same problem saying no that I do."

"Sounds good to me, Dad. Why don't you do that?"

"Dadgoneitall, Dirty Dog! You're getting a little too assertive. I'm not sure that's good for our relationship!"

"Just trying to help, Dad, and I think I've demonstrated over these years that I do want to help you have fun and be a better, more productive man and dad."

"OK, Dirty Dog, point well taken. However, I need to ask you a question."

"OK, Dad, what is it?"

"Is it because you so love to go to the lake that you are encouraging me to go more often?"

"Could be, Dad. Just thought you'd never catch on. But if you want to go and Mom wants to go and I want to go and you get more done, why on earth would you accuse me of having an ulterior motive?"

"OK, Dirty Dog, I surrender. You win hands down. I promise that this year we will go to the lake far more often."

"That's kind of a nebulous answer, Dad. You need to be more specific—like I've heard you tell some of your friends and people who call for advice, 'Be specific!'"

"OK, Dirty Dog. Here's what we'll do. We'll spend at least two days, maybe three days each month next year at the lake."

"Is that a promise, Dad?" "Yes, it is, Dirty Dog. You can tell your mother that's the game plan."

"OK, Dad, I won't say any more about it. However, the first month that you don't keep this commitment, you'll hear from me!"

"Now you're sounding like my mother, Dirty Dog! When we were children she always clearly told us what she expected from us. Then she would always inspect to make certain she had gotten what she expected."

"Good strategy, isn't it, Dad? That's exactly what I intend to do."

"OK, let's close the subject, Dirty Dog. We've worked this one as much as we can, and I believe as much as our readers would be interested in."

Misunderstandings are taken care of when honest communication occurs. Persist. Hang in there until all parties understand one another.

Chapter 11

TV and a Balanced Life

The other day Dirty Dog said, "Dad, I just want to talk. I notice that you and Mom very frequently just sit around and talk, whether you're out in the backyard at sunset, in the house in the den, or sitting around the breakfast table. I know I'd enjoy conversation like that, and I have some questions I really want to ask you."

Since he was obviously sincere about what he was saying, I said, "OK, Dirty Dog, whatcha got on your mind?"

He said, "Well, Dad, I've heard you talk about your childhood—how you are from a family of twelve and you were the tenth to come along, and how things were pretty hard since your dad died when you were just five years old and the country was having some tough economic times. I've heard you talk about working in the grocery store and having a paper route and working in the garden and milking cows and all those things, but, Dad, what did you do to have fun?"

Well, that was a good question because it is true that we all need some rest and relaxation and entertainment, and in those days there were no television sets. Our family didn't even own a radio, but we didn't give much thought to it; we just found fun wherever it was. I explained to Dirty Dog that my mother had a really neat sense of humor and that everybody in the family could find something funny in almost any situation. Then I told him about a little trick my older brothers and sisters had played on me.

Being from the country, we'd never seen or heard of anything called a "doughnut," and when one of my older brothers went to work in the city he bought some of them at the bakery. They were big and they were only fifteen cents a dozen, so he brought each of us one of those doughnuts. As I started to take my first bite (and I believe I was six at that time), two of my older brothers collaborated and told me it would kill me if I ate the hole in the doughnut. I believed them, but I sure wanted that doughnut, so I ate as carefully as a child can eat around that hole, taking special care not to break into that circle because I certainly didn't want to die. I left a little circular morsel of what I perceived as being the most delicious food I'd ever had in my life. I don't think it's necessary to tell you that my brothers were in stitches in another room as they watched me eat that doughnut so carefully.

Then Dirty Dog said, "Well, Dad, don't you think that was a little mean?" I responded that at the time I thought it was a terrible trick to play on me! But I'm sure glad they did, because, in retrospect, it was funny and even today, over seventy years later, I remember and laugh about it. We had fun doing things like that.

"But, Dad, that was just one little five-minute incident. That doesn't make a lifetime of fun, does it?"

And I said, "No, Dirty Dog, it doesn't, but we didn't feel like we had to be entertained all the time as kids are today." And then I explained to Dirty Dog that today the typical 18-year-old has watched 17,000 hours of television, listened to 11,000 hours of music, viewed 2,000 hours of MTV and movies, and this doesn't even include time spent on the telephone, riding around, attending social and athletic events, and the other things teenagers today do.

"When you add it all up, Dirty Dog, it totals over 30,000 hours of being entertained. Now the sad thing is that in 30,000 hours you could finish kindergarten, grade school, middle school, high school, college, medical school and serve an internship—which seems to me to be a better use of time. Now, don't misunderstand, Dirty Dog, I think it's important—even critical—that we have a certain amount of rest, relaxation, and entertainment. But when you've been entertained that amount of time, an interesting phenomenon takes place. Ask any parent of a 'typical teenager' today what they would say is the most standard completion of the following sentence by their teen: 'I am __. There is __ __ __.' I can guarantee that most parents would add the words 'bored' and 'nothing to do.'"

Then Dirty Dog asked a question that many parents have asked: "Why do you think that is?"

"Well, Dirty Dog, I'm convinced that when kids can receive professional entertainment through television and video games, their natural curiosity enters the picture and they laugh, have a good time, marvel at what they're seeing, and are encouraged to participate within the framework of the activity in which they are engaged. In short, it is a programmed type of entertainment, so when children are left on their own they don't know what to do. Most parents will tell you that at Christmastime when the affluent and sometimes the not-so-affluent shower their kids with a large assortment of games and toys, the kids end up playing with the boxes because it allows them to use their creative imaginations to build a fort, dig a tunnel, have an escape hatch, or whatever comes to their minds. When you remove those creativity factors and put them in front of television or a computer game, creativity diminishes, boredom sets in, they don't know what to do, and that's when the foundation for conflict is laid. Kids don't know what to do, parents don't know why they don't know what to do, and you have a never-ending cycle."

"OK, Dad, you've identified the problem," Dirty Dog said. "What's the solution?"

"A couple of things would be extremely helpful, Dirty Dog. Number one, seriously restrict the amount of TV time and then watch TV with the kids to make certain that what they're seeing is neither violent nor obscene. If something negative slips in in the form of a commercial, turn the set off and explain to the child why that is not good and then continue the program. Research conclusively proves that children are far more interested in what Mom or Dad has to say than the other things. It forms a bond that will carry throughout most, if not all, of their lives."

"Is that the reason you and your children are so close today, Dad, and why you work with them, worship with them, vacation with them, eat with them, talk with them on the phone, etc., frequently?"

"Well, it's certainly a factor, Dirty Dog. But I think most of all it's because Mom and I have repeatedly told our kids how much we love them and, perhaps even more important, we have shared our love with and for each other. They have frequently seen us holding hands, hugging and, in general, being nice to each other. Kids have a great sense of security when they know that Mom and Dad are united as one and that they will never have to choose between living with Mom or living with Dad. As a matter of fact, Dirty Dog, each of our children has told us that very thing on numerous occasions, how important it is that they have been able to see that we love each other. Psychologists say the most important thing a father can do for his kids is to love their mother, and the most important thing a mother can do for her kids is to love their father.

"One more thing, Dirty Dog, that I think is important, is that at mealtime there should be absolutely no TV. Once the meal is over, a few minutes spent reading a short devotional thought or story that teaches values and moral lessons, bringing the kids in on the conversation by asking them what they think about it, and then permitting them to express themselves openly is an extremely valuable tool in the parenting process. Lively family discussions are some of the healthiest things families can do."

"Makes sense to me, Dad. A family can't have fun together if they don't spend time together."

The day had been absolutely perfect. I had awakened early, had a very productive morning before the Redhead and even the Dirty Dog were awake. We had an absolutely delightful breakfast, read the paper, and I headed back to my office to continue my writing. I produced some newspaper columns and made a few important phone calls. Lunch at one of our favorite restaurants was particularly pleasant. I received news that our sales staff had been unusually productive that day, making several big sales and numerous little ones, putting life-changing material in the hands of many people.

Later in the afternoon Dirty Dog and I had a really neat walk. I went over to the club and hit golf balls for a few minutes, came back home for more writing, and had a delightful dinner with the Redhead. It was just a beautiful and enjoyable day for me.

At the end of the day Dirty Dog cornered me again. "Dad, you know today has really been a fun day. You and Mom have both been in an unusually good frame of mind; we spent time together, and as I've reflected on these last few months I've come to know more and more why you put so much emphasis on living a balanced life. But it still escapes me just a little, Dad, what you mean by a 'balanced life.'"

This gave me an opportunity to explain something that I should have explained to Dirty Dog long ago, so I responded, "Well, Dirty Dog, research shows that if standard of living is your number one priority in life, the quality of your life seldom improves. But if quality of life is your number one objective, standard of living invariably goes up. My friend Dr. John Maxwell often reminds us that we can live our life any way we want, but we can live it only once, so we do need a good, solid game plan. You might remember that we talked about that on another occasion.

"You see, Dirty Dog, we are physical, mental, and spiritual. In order to get more of the things money will buy (while remembering that money is not the most important thing in life, but it is reasonably close to oxygen), we must understand that we can get everything money buys without character or balance, but we can't get anything money won't buy without character." So the Dirty Dog asked what I meant and I explained to him that my research shows that everyone, regardless of where they live or what they do, wants to be happy, healthy, and at least reasonably prosperous. They want to be secure, have friends, peace of mind, good family relationships, and the hope that the future is going to be even better. They also need to love and to be loved.

"Once we've identified those things, Dirty Dog, we need to bring it all into balance because everything affects everything else. Your personal life affects your family life; your family life affects your physical well-being; your physical well-being affects your mental state. In other words, we do not live in a vacuum. We cannot isolate one phase of our life from another phase."

Then I went ahead to explain that the person who goes to work every morning and the person who comes home in the evening is exactly the same person. Years ago two presidential candidates debated "family values" and never could identify them—because there is no such thing as "family values." "You see, Dirty Dog," I said, "the qualities that make a person a good husband or wife or parent are the same qualities that will make that individual a good boss or employee. There are different skills involved at home and on the job, but the character qualities are always important, regardless of where you are. In order to have a balanced life, you've got to plan for that balanced life.

"One of my favorite examples that I cover in my books and my talks is what I call my 'day before vacation attitude.' The world over, Dirty Dog, people get more work done on the day before they go on vacation than they normally do because the night before that day before vacation they develop a game plan for that last day. Then they make the commitment to follow through, accept the responsibility for performing so they do not leave unfinished things behind for their associates to do, showing that they care about them, and then the next day they arrive promptly, if not a little early, immediately get started, and work with enthusiasm. They stay focused on the task at hand; they do not stop for idle chitchat.

"Most workers tell me they've noticed that as a general rule people with nothing to do want to do it with them. It's amazing how much time you waste in two-minute stops for visits—three minutes here, four minutes there, so by the end of the day at least an hour of your time has been absolutely wasted. That's five hours a week, two hundred fifty hours a year, or *six full weeks* down the drain! But really, Dirty Dog, it's at least twice that much, because that idle chatter involves at least one other person and sometimes more, but even if it's only one person that's two hours a day that's just blown away! But on the day before vacation that doesn't happen. Think what it would mean, Dirty Dog, if we treated every day like the day before vacation. We would get so much more done, move up in the ranks, and be happier in the process.

"Not only that, but there is the satisfaction that goes with doing a good job and knowing that you've been productive. When you get home you just feel so good, you're a better husband, wife, parent, friend, etc. Personally speaking, Dirty Dog, if I did nothing but work and became the richest man in the world but had a very unhappy wife and disgruntled children who ended up as druggies or alcoholics, just how successful would I really be? If I became the best in the whole world at what I do, but destroyed my health in the process, just how successful would I be?"

Well, I noticed as I was sharing these things with Dirty Dog, that he was smiling and nodding his head yes, he agreed with me. Then I elaborated by saying, "As you know, Dirty Dog, not only do I love your mother completely, but she has been enormously helpful to me in my personal life as well as in my career. I often tell people that had it not been for her I certainly would not have enjoyed the success I have enjoyed in the profession I have chosen. We are happy and successful in our life together because we are perfectly balanced. She was the fifth smartest in a class of four hundred, and I was in the part of the class that made the top half possible. This balance enables us to get along exceptionally well.

"When you think about it for a moment, Dirty Dog, if we planned every day as we plan our day before vacation, just think how much more we could get done! Then consider this: If planning one day has such a huge impact on your life, think what planning your life would accomplish. Suppose we planned our family time, planned our personal growth time, our recreation time, our exercise time. Now I mention all of these things, Dirty Dog, because if you will notice (and you've been around long enough to have observed everything), we do all of these things as a family with our children and grandchildren. And the children—you know Julie, our youngest daughter, is the editor of my books; Tom, our son, is the president and CEO of our company; Richard Oates, our son-in-law (married to Cindy), is our chief operating officer. Our other son-in-law, Jim Norman (Julie's husband), serves as a consultant and advisor to the company. Cindy is very supportive of Richard and her dad, and her thing in life, which she loves to do, is to take 'Dr. Emmitt' to hospitals where he serves as a therapy dog. One year, Dirty Dog, as you recall, Cindy was recognized as the 'Volunteer of the Year' in the animal therapy division for all of her service work.

"In addition to working together, we play together, vacation together, do Bible studies together. So, in other words, because we have balance in life we are able to do many more things and be much happier in the process. All of us need to love and be loved. But to be loved, Dirty Dog, as you've heard me say, you've got to be the right kind of person and do the right things in order to have all that life has to offer."

All of this seemed to please Dirty Dog and cleared up many questions about why I take the time I do to talk with and hug on his Mom, and why I spend time on the telephone talking with my children. As a matter of fact, every time I head for the airport I call each one and identify it as their "airport call." When I get back in town I again use my cell phone to call each one with an "airport call," telling them I am home. "In short, Dirty Dog, we stay in close contact, and that's the reason we're close today."

Yes, with forethought, good planning, and good choices, even the busiest schedules can be balanced.

Chapter 12

Scouts and Organ Donors

Why the Boy Scouts?

One afternoon Dirty Dog and I had been having a nice little visit when he said, "Dad, there's something I've been curious about. I know you used to be a Boy Scout; I know you're excited about Scouting; I know you serve on the national board of advisors and have for several years, but, Dad, as busy as you are (and you appear to be getting busier!), why do you take the time to serve the Scouts?"

I said to the Dirty Dog, "I'm glad you asked because the Boy Scouts are very meaningful to me. I believe in what they do with all my heart." I went on to explain that as important as our educational structure is, it leaves out some very important things. Now, don't misunderstand. I think we all must strive to get a solid and balanced formal education. I often tell kids that if they will learn to love to read, they can learn anything they want to know—provided, of course, they read informative, inspirational, educational, valuable materials. But sometimes it's difficult

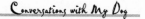

to find the kind of reading materials that will build strong, morally sound, productive, committed young people, and Scouting can be enormously helpful in that light.

His next question was an obvious one, "How does Scouting help do all those things?"

My explanation was, I hope, very clear. I said, "Well, Dirty Dog, as I've explained before, I got busy at a young age and did not have the opportunity to pursue Scouting as far as I would have liked, but I did become a Star Scout, and the things I learned were extremely important."

"Like what, Dad?" he asked.

"Well, you know, the Boy Scout motto is 'Be Prepared.' That's good advice, and it means to be prepared for emergencies, be prepared for life, be prepared to serve—just any number of things, Dirty Dog."

He said, "Well, that does sound like good advice, Dad. What else?"

"In Scouts we are taught to do a good deed every day. That really is the way to win friends and influence people, as you learn to serve others. That's something we all need to know and do." Again, Dirty Dog nodded his approval. Then I said, "Maybe, Dirty Dog, the fact that we have a Scout oath and a Scout law is most important, because they specifically teach how to develop the qualities that make anyone successful in any area of life while bringing balance to life and enabling them to be better parents, husbands, employees, employers, citizens, or, for that matter, serve the government in either a political capacity or a civil service job. The reality, Dirty Dog, is you've got to be the right kind of person, you've got to do the right things in order to have all that life has to offer. And the foundational qualities that Scouting teaches will enable those youngsters to build that foundation.

"For example, the Scout oath. When you stand up and say, 'On my honor . . .' Oh! That's such a beautiful word! . . . 'I will do my best . . .' Now that is good advice, regardless of what you're doing! 'To do my duty to God and my country . . .' That's so important, Dirty Dog! . . . 'And to obey the Scout law . . .' Man alive! That's powerful! . . . 'To help other people at all times. To keep myself physically strong, mentally awake, and morally straight.' I can guarantee you, Dirty Dog, that when young people do those things they are well on their way to developing the qualities that will make them successful.

"But listen to this, the Scout law: 'A Scout is trustworthy, loyal, helpful, friendly, courteous, kind.' Now you think about it, Dirty Dog. As I enumerate these qualities, don't you love to be in this house because you know you can trust us? That we are loyal to you? That we help you, that we are friendly to you, that we are courteous and kind to you? Think about it, Dirty Dog. Well, people are the same way. Part of the law is a Scout is obedient, cheerful, thrifty, brave, clean, and reverent. I'll guarantee you, Dirty Dog, anybody with all of those qualities that they apply on a daily basis will, in fact, be successful and have a balanced life.

"But, Dirty Dog, we've got some results that verify this fact. Judge Elvin Brown up in Norman, Oklahoma, has been on the bench over twenty years. He says that in all those years he's never had a youngster in front of him in court who had spent even one year in Scouting—not even one time! In other words, young people learn in Scouting to be trustworthy and obedient, and to obey the law. Boy, now Dirty Dog, that really says something, doesn't it?

"Let me give you some other results. Kids who stay in Scouting for five years are nearly twice as likely to finish college and nearly three times as likely to earn over $50,000 a year. Now that's important. I guarantee you, Dirty Dog, if I was a young father I would definitely have my boys in Scouting, especially if I were a single parent. But we're not through, Dirty Dog. There are so many other benefits that go with Scouting. Ninety-four percent of those who stay in Scouting for five years stated as adults that the values they learned in Scouting had stood them in good stead all of their lives.

"The research also shows that kids need friends—a group to be part of. They need to receive recognition like I did when I was a youngster and a Boy Scout. Every

Thursday night we'd go to Scout meetings, stand and say that Scout oath and the Scout law, and it made a huge impression on us. But the most exciting night happened once each month. We had what we called the court of honor. That's when we were called up front and merit badges were pinned on us, and when we received promotions, whether it was to Second Class Scout, First Class Scout, Star Scout, Life Scout, right on up the ladder, the recognition was even more significant. Parents frequently attended on court of honor nights to see us get that recognition.

"All kids like to be recognized, and in Scouting we were getting recognition. But listen to this! Ninety-seven percent of kids in Cub Scouting said it was more fun than they expected it to be; 95 percent said they developed new skills; 95 percent said they learned to respect the feelings of others; 98 percent said they felt they were in a friendly, safe environment; 95 percent said it helped them develop social skills; 95 percent said they learned moral, ethical values; 96 percent said they were with positive role models in Scouting. And 97 percent said Scouting enabled them to develop greater father-son togetherness, 94 percent said it helped them to gain a friendly discipline, and 98 percent, Dirty Dog, said it was even better than watching television!

"Now, Dirty Dog, just think about it. If every child in America had a chance to spend five years in Scouting, what a different world we would have. One of the other fringe benefits is that if a Scout troop meets in a church, as I did in the Episcopal Church when I was a youngster, 12 percent of kids who are exposed to Scouting in a church environment join the church and 2 percent of them actually go into ministry of some kind to serve their fellowman. That's the reason, Dirty Dog, I encourage everybody to get involved in Scouting. That's the reason I remain active in it. I believe it is some of the best, most productive time I spend.

"I can tell you, Dirty Dog, that one of the most meaningful recognitions I have ever received is the Silver Buffalo Award that was presented to me in October 2002. I was told that, created in 1925, this award is 'bestowed upon those who give truly noteworthy and extraordinary service to youth.' It's considered Scouting's highest commendation and 'recognizes the invaluable contributions that outstanding American men and women render to youth.' Other recipients have been Lord Robert Baden-Powell, founder of the Scouting movement and chief Scout of the world; Charles A. Lindbergh; Norman Rockwell; General Colin L. Powell; Apollo 13 commander James A. Lovell, Jr.; Walt Disney; Hank Aaron; Bob Hope; Vince Lombardi; Neil Armstrong; Charles M. Schulz; and thirteen presidents of the United States, among others. I tell you, I feel like I'm in pretty tall cotton when I look at that list! But why I feel so privileged by the recognition is the purpose of the award most of all, and I was truly honored and humbled by it.

"Well, Dirty Dog, I know it sounded like I was on a pretty big soapbox there, but our character is truly important! These character qualities will serve Scouts all of their lives in every way imaginable."

Well, I've got to admit that as Dirty Dog was nodding his head in agreement with what I was saying, I was very pleased. And when it was all over he said, "Well, Dad, that might have been a little more than I wanted to know about it, but I'm glad you took the time to tell me. Now I understand why you're always encouraging parents to involve their kids in Scouting."

Six Transplants

I never cease to be amazed at the subjects Dirty Dog brings up and some of the conversations we have. On February 22, 2002, I had my third attack of diverticulitis and ended up having 75 percent of my colon removed after losing six pints of blood. I spent nine days in the hospital. When I returned home, Dirty Dog greeted me with "happy eyes" and indicated that he really had missed me— and that always pleases me. However, I was still fairly weak and in no mood to talk, so I asked him to hold his questions and a little later I would be happy to answer them.

Reluctantly he agreed and waited patiently several days before his demeanor indicated he just had to talk.

I opened the conversation with, "OK, Dirty Dog, whatcha got on your mind?"

He responded, "Well, Dad, I missed you those nine days and wanted to talk with you because ever since I heard about Richard's liver transplant I've been curious as to what that was all about. Now I understand you had six 'transplants' while you were in the hospital."

Obviously, the subject did require some explanation so I explained that Rich had hepatitis C and his liver was no longer functioning as it should, so he had gotten on the waiting list to receive a liver transplant. I told him that if he had not received a transplant, Rich might have died by now and would have made his trip into eternity. Not that he'd mind eternity, but he's looking forward to doing some more things here on Earth. I explained to the Dirty Dog that the young donor, Matthew McCord, was killed when his car ran off a dangerous stretch of rain-slick highway and therefore had no further use for his liver. And I told him there was a lot more to the story!

I explained that the gracious generosity of Matthew McCord and his family went far beyond Richard's liver transplant. As a very young man, Matthew McCord became almost obsessed with the idea that whenever possible, organs should be donated so that others might live.

His mother even told Cindy that every Christmas Matthew would go around asking different members of the family if they'd gotten their organ donor cards yet. His passion to promote organ donation made it abundantly clear to his family what he would want them to do, so when he died Matthew's heart, lungs, pancreas, and kidneys were also donated. Today five people are alive because of this young man's commitment to the transplant program.

Dirty Dog said, "I understand about Rich now, Dad. What happened to you?"

I explained that saying I had six "transplants" was a slight stretch because what I received was six pints of blood, all from living donors. The blood probably did come from six different donors, but had that blood not been available at that critical moment when my need was great, there is a good chance I would now be spending eternity with my Lord and my loved ones who've gone ahead of me. Because of those six units that were transfused into my body, I'm enjoying marvelous health; I'm operating on a full schedule and looking forward to an exciting future.

I explained to Dirty Dog that the Redhead has also had two transplants. They were cornea transplants and have kept her from going blind due to an inherited disease called Fuchs' Dystrophy. Then I'll have to confess I got on my soapbox and explained that people should make their desire to donate their organs clear to their family. They also need to wear the green donor ribbon to promote being an organ donor. Organ donation truly is unselfish, and yet you give up absolutely nothing because when you die, you obviously have no need or use for your organs.

It is impossible to describe the feelings of gratitude that Rich and Cindy have for this beautiful family who, recognizing their son/husband/brother was no longer with them, wanted to fulfill his wish. Today they are all good friends, and over the years chances are good that friendship will continue to grow. I can say with conviction that the gratitude Cindy and Richard feel, as well as the rest of the family, knows no limits.

To be honest, when the conversation was over, Dirty Dog was very quiet. He finally commented that he was glad Rich was able to get that liver transplant, that the other recipients were able to use the other donated organs to sustain their lives, and that his mom can see better because of her cornea transplants. And he even said, "Dad, I'm glad you're going to be around a while longer because somebody donated blood." This is something serious to think about, and I'm glad Dirty Dog brought the subject up and gave me a chance to express myself.

Note to the Reader: In my own life, my gratitude bucket runs over, as does the Redhead's, for the transplants we have received. Modern medicine really does offer some tremendous advantages and hope for the future. I hope Dirty Dog made the connection between the two topics covered in this chapter. The principles taught in Scouting are the very principles that make people willing to be organ donors. I hope everyone who reads this book, who is in a position to do so, will make it clear that in the event of a sudden death, his or her organs are to be donated to those who can use them.

Another note that I'm so blessed to add here is that Richard's liver has undoubtedly extended his life and improved the quality of his life.

Chapter 13

Making Big Decisions

Our home at Holly Lake in East Texas is our favorite place to go when we have a couple of days we can call our own. This is where I do some of my writing, a lot of walking, relaxing, and occasionally play some golf. One afternoon when my daughter Cindy was visiting us at the lake we decided to take a long walk. Dirty Dog and his buddy, Emmitt, were our companions.

Cindy has a favorite place to walk at the lake. Getting there necessitates crossing a small wooded area and a small tree-lined road. It doesn't take us long to reach the less-developed land where we have a better chance of seeing an occasional deer, raccoon, armadillo, rabbit, squirrel, or even a skunk. We had committed to a long walk because in that area we can let the dogs run free and they really enjoy that! However, when we crossed the little road we saw for the first time a "posted" sign. I laughingly said, "Well, that certainly doesn't mean us!" and immediately thought to myself, "but it really *does* mean us." We debated back and forth and finally Cindy said, "It's up to you, Dad. What do you want to do?" With that I started a little dissertation that included the fact that there might be hunters in there and if we should encounter one our chances of being accidentally shot would not make for a very pleasant experience.

Then my life-saving decision maker surfaced again, and I said, "Well, the question is, 'What would Jesus do?'" We knew that He would never go where He had been warned not to go in violation of the law. So we reluctantly stayed on the road and since there was zero traffic that was not a major sacrifice.

As we walked, Dirty Dog spoke up for the first time and said, "Dad, I wasn't really paying attention when you and Cindy were talking about why we didn't go into that lush area where Emmitt and I have so much fun. But you seem to be satisfied with the choice you made, even though you never consulted with me or Emmitt. I'm puzzled, Dad. Why did you make that decision?"

I explained to Dirty Dog my line of thinking. When I finished my explanation, saying that I wanted to try to make important decisions with the question, "What would Jesus do?" he said, "Well, Dad, that sure makes sense to me, and I want you to know that I understand and bear no hard feelings toward you." Then he paused for a moment and said, "But, Dad, I do have a couple of questions," and I said, "Sure, Dirty Dog, shoot."

He said, "Dad, do you always follow that process?"

I had to confess that no, sometimes I go through the human process and make decisions in other ways.

Then he quizzed me by asking, "On which occasions do you ask, 'What would Jesus do?'"

I said, "Well, Dirty Dog, I do that when the decisions are really important and reflect on a person's integrity or can affect anything of any significance."

Then he said, "Well, Dad, do you ever ask what would Jesus do when you start to dip out that small portion of food you and Mom give me twice each day?"

I had to confess to Dirty Dog that no, I never asked what would Jesus do when it came to feeding him.

He said, "Well, Dad, that might not be very important to you, but it's very important to me. I wish you would ask Him, because I believe He would tell you to give me lots more than you are giving me."

To that I responded, "No, Dirty Dog, I don't think He would," and for the first time I realized just how much theology Dirty Dog had absorbed in the eight-plus years he had been in our home. He explained to me that Jesus was always giving more than was expected and that He apparently loved dogs because He and His Father and the Holy Spirit created lots of dogs and, for that matter, all kinds of animals, and "I'll bet He doesn't want to see them mistreated!"

For a moment Dirty Dog had taken the debating edge, but then I responded to Dirty Dog by saying, "Well, Dirty Dog, one of the things Jesus has taught me in dealing not only with people but with our four-legged friends is that when we have decisions to make regarding them we should always make them in their own best interests."

Dirty Dog responded, "Well, don't you think it's in my best interests to have enough to eat?"

I said, "Yes, Dirty Dog, but you get enough to eat. According to the veterinarian, if we give you too much to eat you will gain weight, and as you know, Dirty Dog, you have an unusually long back. If that stomach of yours is overextended, it will work a hardship on your back. Then you couldn't run, play, and wrestle with Emmitt, and you'd be restricted to short walks instead of the long walks we usually take. Not only that, but you'd have to take more trips to the vet, get more shots, and put up with all the exploring they do. And, Dirty Dog, we've already discovered that you don't really look forward to those trips to the vet."

Then Dirty Dog acknowledged that it did appear that we were acting in his best interests and even expressed appreciation for it as he acknowledged that no, he was not particularly fond of going to see the vet, although he was certain the vet meant well.

All in all, it was a very enlightening and informative conversation, and I came away from it feeling that the Dirty Dog and I now had a better understanding of each other.

Understanding

Speaking of understanding, Dirty Dog is a stickler about understanding things. One day he said, "Dad, I overhead a conversation you were having with Mom."

I asked, "What conversation was that, Dirty Dog?"

He responded, "Well, just a few minutes ago, while you were drinking your coffee you told Mom you couldn't imagine anyone being any happier than you. You told her how much you enjoyed church but that you had lots of memories of Suzan when the little children came forward with their parents to commit their lives to Christ and join the church. I just sensed, Dad, that you really needed someone to talk to."

"I believe you're exactly right, Dirty Dog. Even though church and Sunday school were most enjoyable, I did get a little weepy when Dr. Graham started talking about *Confessions of a Grieving Christian.* You know, writing that book about the grief I felt when Suzan died is probably one of the toughest things I've ever done in my life. And working on it at the same time I was trying to meet the publisher's deadline for *Success for Dummies* really added to the strain of it all. I guess listening to Dr. Graham talk about the book today just brought it all back to me. As each of those little children accepted Christ as their Lord and Savior this morning, I wondered if they were going to get to know Suzan in heaven one day.

"I really appreciate you taking the time to listen to your old Dad, Dirty Dog. I had no idea you were so compassionate and sensitive to my needs."

"Well, Dad, I have been around for several years now, and I've come to know you well. I've watched and listened to you and though I've always spent more time with Mom, I feel like I know you as well or better than almost anyone."

"Well, Dirty Dog, I appreciate that very much. Truthfully, I did enjoy and need the talk."

"OK, Dad, now you can listen to me for a few minutes. All this talk about Suzan really makes me miss her. She went home to be with the Lord so many years ago and it seems to me like only yesterday. That brings up a couple of questions, Dad. I've heard you talk, and I've heard the family talk, and everybody is completely convinced that she is in heaven with Jesus. Dad, I've never really studied the Bible; I've only listened to what you and the rest of the family say, but how can you be so certain that she is in heaven?"

"Well, Dirty Dog, fortunately, God assigned many different men to write all the books of the Bible. They wrote it in three different languages, on three different continents, over a span of 1,500 years. But they wrote under the guidance of the Holy Spirit. It's almost like God dictated the letters Himself, but really it was inspiration of thoughts, and He allowed each one of these men to inject their own personalities into their writing. But we know it had to come from God, Dirty Dog, because there are over 60 major prophecies and 270 ramifications about the birth, death, and resurrection of Jesus Christ, all of which were written at least 400 years before His birth, and all of them have come to pass exactly as prophesied. (For further elaboration, read Josh McDowell's small book, *More than a Carpenter.*)

"I give you that background, Dirty Dog, so you will be able to follow me on why we're so confident that Suzan is in heaven. First we know she's there because in Ephesians 2:8–9 we read, 'For it is by grace you have been saved through faith—and this not from yourselves, it is the gift of God—not by works—so that no one can boast' (NIV). In other words, Dirty Dog, it's not what Suzan did, though she was a wonderful daughter and a wonderful woman, but it's what Christ did for her that got her to heaven."

"Well, Dad, exactly what did He do for her?"

"Well, John 3:16 tells us that 'God so loved the world that He gave His only begotten Son, that whoever believes in Him should not perish but have everlasting life'" (NKJV).

"What does that mean, Dad?"

"It simply means that Jesus went to the cross and that His blood was shed. His blood washed away Suzan's sins so we know that she is in heaven."

"But, Dad, what did Suzan have to do?"

"Well, God tells us in Romans 10:9, 'If you confess with your mouth the Lord Jesus and believe in your heart that God has raised Him from the dead, you will be saved' (NKJV). And, Dirty Dog, I can tell you that Suzan did exactly that. She believed in her heart that Jesus was Lord. And she believed that God raised Him from death. She was saved and is now in heaven. As a matter of fact, Christ said while He was on earth, 'I go before you to prepare a place for you; in my house are many mansions. If it were not so, I would have told you so.' So, Dirty Dog, Jesus went before and prepared that place for Suzan."

"You mean that's all she had to do?"

"Yes, it is, Dirty Dog, because in John 14:6 we read, 'Jesus said, "I am the way, the truth, and the life. No one comes to the Father except through Me"'" (NKJV).

"You mean she didn't have to do any work to get there?"

"No, Dirty Dog. In John 6:29 it clearly says, 'This is the work of God: that you believe in the One He has sent'" (HCSB).

"Well, Dad, that sounds almost too good to be true!"

"Yes, it is almost too good to be true! But we have a God who cannot lie. The Bible tells us that Jesus Christ is the same yesterday, today, and forever. He did that for us, Dirty Dog, not because we deserve it but because He loves us. In other words, it's not what we do; it's what He did that gets us to heaven."

"Then my question is, since Suzan is in heaven, why did we have that funeral and why is she buried out at the cemetery?"

"Well, Dirty Dog, only her earthly body is there. We have funerals and burials to show respect and reverence for the life of the one who has passed. But Suzan's spirit, her soul, is in heaven with Jesus."

"I want to be in heaven, too! Is there a place there for dogs?"

"Well, Dirty Dog, from what I read in Revelation 5:13–14, I think you can count on being there, along with Emmitt and even the bad dogs, because the Bible says, 'Every creature in heaven and on earth . . .' (NIV), and it even says you'll have a voice! You'll be proclaiming, 'To Him who sits on the throne, and to the Lamb, be praise and honor and glory and power forever and ever.' I can't imagine heaven being heaven without you, Dirty Dog, and apparently God couldn't either. You're so much fun here that I just believe there's a place for you up there."

"Dad, do you have any more evidence to support that?"

"The Lord told us that one day the lion will lay down with the lamb. And if the lion is going to lay down with the lamb, where would they be? I've got to believe, Dirty Dog, that there will be little dogs like you and big dogs like Emmitt who are going to be right there. I believe God surely loves you and Emmitt and the other dogs as much as He does the lion. And though symbolically speaking, Christ is the 'lamb of God,' and the lamb was used in the feast of the Passover, I believe you rate fully as high on the totem pole as the lion or the lamb. In short, Dirty Dog, I believe you and I are going to have an ongoing relationship for a long time."

"That's comforting to know, Dad. I don't understand a lot of what you're saying, but I do trust you to tell me the truth."

Being a dog does inhibit Dirty Dog's ability to understand spiritual things to a degree, but God made you and me with a built-in desire to know Him. If you aren't sure about your relationship with Him and you want to know more, write me at:

Ziglar Training Systems
15303 Dallas Parkway, Suite 55
Addison, Texas 75001
www.ziglartraining.com

In Closing

I believe that one of the saddest facts of my life is that our dog friends live a life that is far too short. From the instant you claim them as your own, but you know that the day you say good-bye will come too soon. In the time since Dirty Dog and I finished this manuscript, both he and his best friend, Emmitt, have died.

I'm grieved to tell you that my coauthor stepped into eternity at noon on June 2, 2003, when his heart stopped and he breathed his last. The grief and sense of loss our family experienced—and continues to experience—has brought forth many tears. His problem was a liver too small, which spawned scores of other health problems. His decline into poor health was long and slow, but the end arrived much too quickly. It was heartbreaking to have to carry Dirty Dog, the personification of energy, up the stairs every night and to watch him being hand-fed by the Redhead. In many ways his premature death at the age of nine was a blessing.

Dirty Dog left a legacy of love, compassion, encouragement, and an unbounded zest for life. He was just shy of a year old when we first brought him home to live with us, and his boisterous antics entertained us from sunup to sundown. Four months later when Suzan died he took on the role of comforter. He witnessed the depth of our grief and sat quietly in our laps, his thick, soft fur absorbing our torrent of tears. His playfulness created a much-needed distraction in the midst of our mourning and helped us maintain sanity and balance in our lives in the aftermath of Suzan's death. We understood fully that he was a gift from God. Just having him to hold in our laps was a blessing that was not lost on us.

Like Dirty Dog we find consolation in the fact that we will be reunited with him in heaven, and all of us look forward to that reunion. We take comfort in the fact that at this moment his energy level is higher than ever; he is feeling no pain, and is having the time of his life as he entertains those who preceded him. We miss him very much but we are grateful that during his short life his contribution to our lives was huge.